CHRONICLES OF CANADA SERIES
THIRTY-TWO VOLUMES ILLUSTRATED
Edited by GEORGE M. WRONG and H. H. LANGTON

CHRONICLES OF CANADA SERIES

NOTE.—Save for slight changes in arrangement and in the words of a few of the titles, this list remains essentially as printed in the prospectus with the twelve volumes first published, and may now be regarded as final. The eight volumes marked with an asterisk, however, are still in preparation and subject to changes in authorship should unforeseen circumstances prevent any author from completing his manuscript.

CHRONICLES OF CANADA SERIES

CHRONICLES OF CANADA SERIES

TORONTO: GLASGOW, BROOK & COMPANY

THE WAR CHIEF OF THE OTTAWAS

BY THOMAS GUTHRIE MARQUIS

THE BLACK WATCH AT BUSHY RUN, 1763

From a colour drawing by C. W. Jefferys

THE WAR CHIEF
OF THE OTTAWAS

A Chronicle of the Pontiac War

BY

THOMAS GUTHRIE MARQUIS

TORONTO

GLASGOW, BROOK & COMPANY

1915

F
10R6
.C45
v.15
1915
Copy 1

CONTENTS

ILLUSTRATIONS

CHAPTER I

THE TIMES AND THE MEN

THERE was rejoicing throughout the Thirteen Colonies, in the month of September 1760, when news arrived of the capitulation of Montreal. Bonfires flamed forth and prayers were offered up in the churches and meeting-houses in gratitude for deliverance from a foe that for over a hundred years had harried and had caused the Indians to harry the frontier settlements. The French armies were defeated by land; the French fleets were beaten at sea. The troops of the enemy had been removed from North America, and so powerless was France on the ocean that, even if success should crown her arms on the European continent, where the Seven Years' War was still raging, it would be impossible for her to transport a new force to America. The principal French forts in America were occupied by British troops. Louisbourg had been razed to the ground; the British flag waved over Quebec, Montreal, and Niagara, and was soon to be raised on all the lesser forts in the territory known as Canada.   The Mississippi valley from the Illinois river southward alone remained to France.   Vincennes on the Wabash and Fort Chartres on the Mississippi were the only posts in the hinterland occupied by French troops.   These posts were under the government of Louisiana ; but even these the American colonies were prepared to claim, basing the right on their ' sea to sea ' charters.

The British in America had found the strip of land between the Alleghanies and the Atlantic far too narrow for a rapidly increasing population, but their advance westward had been barred by the French.   Now, praise the Lord, the French were out of the way, and American traders and settlers could exploit the profitable fur-fields and the rich agricultural lands of the region beyond the mountains.   True, the Indians were there, but these were not regarded as formidable foes.   There was no longer any occasion to consider the Indians—so thought the colonists and the British officers in America.   The red men had been a force to be reckoned with only because the French had supplied them with the sinews of war, but they might now be treated like other denizens of the forest—the bears, the wolves, and the wild cats. For this mistaken policy the British colonies were to pay a heavy price.

The French and the Indians, save for one exception, had been on terms of amity from the beginning. The reason for this was that the French had treated the Indians with studied kindness. The one exception was the Iroquois League or Six Nations. Champlain, in the first years of his residence at Quebec, had joined the Algonquins and Hurons in an attack on them, which they never forgot; and, in spite of the noble efforts of French missionaries and a lavish bestowal of gifts, the Iroquois thorn remained in the side of New France. But with the other Indian tribes the French worked hand in hand, with the Cross and the priest ever in advance of the trader's pack. French missionaries were the first white men to settle in the populous Huron country near Lake Simcoe. A missionary was the first European to catch a glimpse of Georgian Bay, and a missionary was probably the first of the French race to launch his canoe on the lordly Mississippi. As a father the priest watched over his wilderness flock; while the French traders fraternized with the red men, and often mated with dusky beauties. Many French traders, according to Sir William Johnson—a good authority, of whom we shall learn more later—were ' gentlemen in manners, character, and dress,' and they treated the natives kindly. At the great centres of trade —Montreal, Three Rivers, and Quebec—the chiefs were royally received with roll of drum and salute of guns. The governor himself —the ' Big Mountain,' as they called him— would extend to them a welcoming hand and take part in their feastings and councils. At the inland trading-posts the Indians were given goods for their winter hunts on credit and loaded with presents by the officials. To such an extent did the custom of giving presents prevail that it became a heavy tax on the treasury of France, insignificant, however, compared with the alternative of keeping in the hinterland an armed force. The Indians, too, had fought side by side with the French in many notable engagements. They had aided Montcalm, and had assisted in such triumphs as the defeat of Braddock. They were not only friends of the French; they were sword companions.

The British colonists could not, of course, entertain friendly feelings towards the tribes which sided with their enemies and often devastated their homes and murdered their people.   But it must be admitted that, from the first, the British in America were far behind the French in christianlike conduct towards the native races.   The colonial traders generally despised the Indians and treated them as of commercial value only, as gatherers of pelts, and held their lives in little more esteem than the lives of the animals that yielded the pelts.   The missionary zeal of New England, compared with that of New France, was exceedingly mild.   Rum was a leading article of trade.   The Indians were often cheated out of their furs ; in some instances they were slain and their packs stolen.   Sir William Johnson described the British traders as ' men of no zeal or capacity: men who even sacrifice the credit of the nation to the basest purposes.'   There were exceptions, of course, in such men as Alexander Henry and Johnson himself, who, besides being a wise official and a successful military commander, was one of the leading traders.

No sooner was New France vanquished than the British began building new forts and

blockhouses in the hinterland.[1] Since the
French were no longer to be reckoned with,
why were these forts needed ? Evidently,
the Indians thought, to keep the red children
in subjection and to deprive them of their
hunting-grounds ! The gardens they saw
in cultivation about the forts were to them
the forerunners of general settlement. The
French had been content with trade ; the
British appropriated lands for farming, and
the coming of the white settler meant the
disappearance of game. Indian chiefs saw
in these forts and cultivated strips of land a
desire to exterminate the red man and steal
his territory ; and they were not far wrong.

Outside influences, as well, were at work
among the Indians. Soon after the French
armies departed, the inhabitants along the
St Lawrence had learned to welcome the
change of government. They were left to
cultivate their farms in peace. The tax-
gatherer was no longer squeezing from them
their last *sou* as in the days of Bigot ; nor were
their sons, whose labour was needed on the
farms and in the workshops, forced to take up

[1] By the hinterland is meant, of course, the regions beyond the
zone of settlement ; roughly, all west of Montreal and the
Alleghanies.

arms. They had peace and plenty, and were content. But in the hinterland it was different. At Detroit, Michilimackinac, and other forts were French trading communities, which, being far from the seat of war and government, were slow to realize that they were no longer subjects of the French king. Hostile themselves, these French traders naturally encouraged the Indians in an attitude of hostility to the incoming British. They said that a French fleet and army were on their way to Canada to recover the territory. Even if Canada were lost, Louisiana was still French, and, if only the British could be kept out of the west, the trade that had hitherto gone down the St Lawrence might now go by way of the Mississippi.

The commander-in-chief of the British forces in North America, Sir Jeffery Amherst, despised the red men. They were ' only fit to live with the inhabitants of the woods, being more nearly allied to the Brute than to the Human creation.' Other British officers had much the same attitude. Colonel Henry Bouquet, on a suggestion made to him by Amherst that blankets infected with small-pox might be distributed to good purpose among the savages, not only fell in with Amherst's views, but further proposed that dogs should be used to hunt them down. ' You will do well,' Amherst wrote to Bouquet, ' to try to inoculate the Indians by means of Blankets as well as to try every other method that can serve to extirpate this Execrable Race. I should be very glad if your scheme for hunting them down by dogs could take effect, but England is at too great a Distance to think of that at present.' And Major Henry Gladwyn, who, as we shall see, gallantly held Detroit through months of trying siege, thought that the unrestricted sale of rum among the Indians would extirpate them more quickly than powder and shot, and at less cost.

There was, however, one British officer, at least, in America who did not hold such views towards the natives of the soil. Sir William Johnson, through his sympathy and generosity, had won the friendship of the Six Nations, the most courageous and the most cruel of the Indian tribes.[1] It has been said by a recent writer that Johnson was ' as much Indian as white man.'[2] Nothing could be more misleading. Johnson was simply an enlightened

---

[1] For more about Sir William Johnson see *The War Chief of the Six Nations* in this Series.

[2] Lucas's *A History of Canada, 1763-1812*, p. 58.

Irishman of broad sympathies who could make himself at home in palace, hut, or wigwam. He was an astute diplomatist, capable of winning his point in controversy with the most learned and experienced legislators of the colonies, a successful military leader, a most successful trader; and there was probably no more progressive and scientific farmer in America.   He had a cultivated mind; the orders he sent to London for books show that he was something of a scholar and in his leisure moments given to serious reading.   His advice to the lords of trade regarding colonial affairs was that of a statesman.   He fraternized with the Dutch settlers of his neighbourhood and with the Indians wherever he found them.   At Detroit, in 1761, he entered into the spirit of the French settlers and joined with enthusiasm in their feasts and dances.   He was one of those rare characters who can be all things to all men and yet keep an untarnished name.   The Indians loved him as a firm friend, and his home was to them Liberty Hall.   But for this man the Indian rising against British rule would have attained greater proportions.   At the critical period he succeeded in keeping the Six Nations loyal, save for the Senecas.   This was most important ; for had the Six Nations joined in the war against the British, it is probable that not a fort west of Montreal would have remained standing. The line of communication between Albany and Oswego would have been cut, provisions and troops could not have been forwarded, and, inevitably, both Niagara and Detroit would have fallen.

But as it was, the Pontiac War proved serious enough. It extended as far north as Sault Ste Marie and as far south as the borders of South Carolina and Georgia. Detroit was cut off for months ; the Indians drove the British from all other points on the Great Lakes west of Lake Ontario ; for a time they triumphantly pushed their war-parties, plundering and burning and murdering, from the Mississippi to the frontiers of New York. During the year 1763 more British lives were lost in America than in the memorable year of 1759, the year of the siege of Quebec and the world-famous battle of the Plains of Abraham.

SIR WILLIAM JOHNSON

From an engraving by Spooner after a painting by Adams

CHAPTER II

PONTIAC AND THE TRIBES OF THE HINTERLAND

FOREMOST among the Indian leaders was Pontiac, the over-chief of the Ottawa Confederacy. It has been customary to speak of this chief as possessed of ' princely grandeur ' and as one ' honoured and revered by his subjects.' But it was not by a display of princely dignity or by inspiring awe and reverence that he influenced his bloodthirsty followers. His chief traits were treachery and cruelty, and his pre-eminence in these qualities commanded their respect. His conduct of the siege of Detroit, as we shall see, was marked by duplicity and diabolic savagery. He has often been extolled for his skill as a military leader, and there is a good deal in his siege of Detroit and in the murderous ingenuity of some of his raids to support this view. But his principal claim to distinction is due to his position as the head of a confederacy—whereas the other chiefs in the conflict were merely leaders of single tribes—and to the fact that he was situated at the very centre of the theatre of war. News from Detroit could be quickly heralded along the canoe routes and forest trails to the other tribes, and it thus happened that when Pontiac struck, the whole Indian country rose in arms. But the evidence clearly shows that, except against Detroit and the neighbouring blockhouses, he had no part in planning the attacks. The war as a whole was a leaderless war.

Let us now look for a moment at the Indians who took part in the war. Immediately under the influence of Pontiac were three tribes—the Ottawas, the Chippewas, and the Potawatomis. These had their hunting-grounds chiefly in the Michigan peninsula, and formed what was known as the Ottawa Confederacy or the Confederacy of the Three Fires. It was at the best a loose confederacy, with nothing of the organized strength of the Six Nations. The Indians in it were of a low type—sunk in savagery and superstition. A leader such as Pontiac naturally appealed to them. They existed by hunting and fishing—feasting to-day and famishing to-morrow—and were easily roused by the hope of plunder. The weakly manned forts containing the white man's provisions, ammunition, and traders' supplies were an attractive lure to such savages. Within the confederacy, however, there were some who did not rally round Pontiac. The Ottawas of the northern part of Michigan, under the influence of their priest, remained friendly to the British. Including the Ottawas and Chippewas of the Ottawa and Lake Superior, the confederates numbered many thousands ; yet at no time was Pontiac able to command from among them more than one thousand warriors.

In close alliance with the Confederacy of the Three Fires were the tribes dwelling to the west of Lake Michigan—the Menominees, the Winnebagoes, and the Sacs and Foxes. These tribes could put into the field about twelve hundred warriors ; but none of them took part in the war save in one instance, when the Sacs, moved by the hope of plunder, assisted the Chippewas in the capture of Fort Michilimackinac.

The Wyandots living on the Detroit river were a remnant of the ancient Hurons of the famous mission near Lake Simcoe. For more than a century they had been bound to the French by ties of amity. They were courage-

ous, intelligent, and in every way on a higher
plane of life than the tribes of the Ottawa
Confederacy.   Their two hundred and fifty
braves were to be Pontiac's most important
allies in the siege of Detroit.

South of the Michigan peninsula, about
the head-waters of the rivers Maumee and
Wabash, dwelt the Miamis, numbering probably about fifteen hundred.   Influenced by
French traders and by Pontiac's emissaries,
they took to the war-path, and the British
were thus cut off from the trade-route between
Lake Erie and the Ohio.

The tribes just mentioned were all that came
under the direct influence of Pontiac.   Farther
south were other nations who were to figure in
the impending struggle.   The Wyandots of
Sandusky Bay, at the south-west corner of
Lake Erie, had about two hundred warriors,
and were in alliance with the Senecas and
Delawares.   Living near Detroit, they were
able to assist in Pontiac's siege.   Directly
south of these, along the Scioto, dwelt the
Shawnees—the tribe which later gave birth
to the great Tecumseh—with three hundred
warriors.   East of the Shawnees, between the
Muskingum and the Ohio, were the Delawares.
At one time this tribe had lived on both

sides of the Delaware river in Pennsylvania
and New York, and also in parts of New
Jersey and Delaware. They called themselves
Leni-Lenape, real men ; but were, nevertheless, conquered by the Iroquois, who ' made
women ' of them, depriving them of the right
to declare war or sell land without permission.
Later, through an alliance with the French,
they won back their old independence. But
they lay in the path of white settlement, and
were ousted from one hunting-ground after
another, until finally they had to seek homes
beyond the Alleghanies. The British had
robbed the Delawares of their ancient lands,
and the Delawares hated with an undying
hatred the race that had injured them. They
mustered six hundred warriors.

Almost directly south of Fort Niagara, by
the upper waters of the Genesee and Alleghany rivers, lay the homes of the Senecas,
one of the Six Nations. This tribe looked
upon the British settlers in the Niagara
region as squatters on their territory. It was
the Senecas, not Pontiac, who began the
plot for the destruction of the British in the
hinterland, and in the war which followed more
than a thousand Seneca warriors took part.
Happily, as has been mentioned, Sir William

Johnson was able to keep the other tribes of the Six Nations loyal to the British; but the ' Door-keepers of the Long House,' as the Senecas were called, stood aloof and hostile.

The motives of the Indians in the rising of 1763 may, therefore, be summarized as follows : amity with the French, hostility towards the British, hope of plunder, and fear of aggression. The first three were the controlling motives of Pontiac's Indians about Detroit. They called it the ' Beaver War.' To them it was a war on behalf of the French traders, who loaded them with gifts, and against the British, who drove them away empty-handed. But the Senecas 'and the Delawares, with their allies of the Ohio valley, regarded it as a war for their lands. Already the Indians had been forced out of their hunting-grounds in the valleys of the Juniata and the Susquehanna. The Ohio valley would be the next to go, unless the Indians went on the war-path. The chiefs there had good reason for alarm. Not so Pontiac at Detroit, because no settlers were invading his hunting-grounds. And it was for this lack of a strong motive that Pontiac's campaign, as will hereafter appear, broke down before the end of the war; that even his own confederates deserted him; and that, while the Senecas and Delawares were still holding out, he was wandering through the Indian country in a vain endeavour to rally his scattered warriors.

CHAPTER III

THE GATHERING STORM

WHEN Montreal capitulated, and the whole of Canada passed into British hands, it was the duty of Sir Jeffery Amherst, the commander-in-chief, to arrange for the defence of the country that had been wrested from France. General Gage was left in command at Montreal, Colonel Burton at Three Rivers, and General Murray at Quebec. Amherst himself departed for New York in October, and never again visited Canada. Meanwhile provision had been made, though quite inadequate, to garrison the long chain of forts [1] that had been established by the French in the vaguely defined Indian territory to the west. The fortunes of war had already given

[1] See the accompanying map. Except for these forts or trading-posts, the entire region west of Montreal was at this time practically an unbroken wilderness. There were on the north shore of the St Lawrence a few scattered settlements, on Île Perrot and at Vaudreuil, and on the south shore at the Cedars and Chateauguay; but anything like continuity of settlement westward ceased with the island of Montreal.

the British command of the eastern end of this chain. Fort Lévis, on what is now Chimney Island, a few miles east of Ogdensburg, had been captured. Fort Frontenac had been destroyed by Bradstreet, and was left without a garrison. British troops were in charge of Fort Oswego, which had been built in 1759. Niagara, the strongest fort on the Great Lakes, had been taken by Sir William Johnson. Near it were two lesser forts, one at the foot of the rapids, where Lewiston now stands, and the other, Fort Schlosser, on the same side of the river, above the falls. Forts Presqu'isle, Le Bœuf, and Venango, on the trade-route between Lake Erie and Fort Pitt, and Fort Pitt itself, were also occupied. But all west of Fort Pitt was to the British unknown country. Sandusky, at the south-west end of Lake Erie; Detroit, guarding the passage between Lakes Erie and St Clair; Miami and Ouiatanon, on the trade-route between Lake Erie and the Wabash; Michilimackinac, at the entrance to Lake Michigan; Green Bay (La Baye), at the southern end of Green Bay; St Joseph, on Lake Michigan; Sault Ste Marie, at the entrance to Lake Superior—all were still commanded by French officers, as they had been under New France.

The task of raising the British flag over these forts was entrusted to Major Robert Rogers of New England, who commanded Rogers's Rangers, a famous body of Indian-fighters. On September 13, 1760, with two hundred Rangers in fifteen whale-boats, Rogers set out from Montreal. On November 7 the contingent without mishap reached a river named by Rogers the Chogage, evidently the Cuyahoga, on the south shore of Lake Erie. Here the troops landed, probably on the site of the present city of Cleveland; and Rogers was visited by a party of Ottawa Indians, whom he told of the conquest of Canada and of the retirement of the French armies from the country. He added that his force had been sent by the commander-in-chief to take over for their father, the king of England, the western posts still held by French soldiers. He then offered them a peace-belt, which they accepted, and re-quested them to go with him to Detroit to take part in the capitulation and 'see the truth' of what he had said. They promised to give him an answer next morning. The calumet was smoked by the Indians and the officers in turn; but a careful guard was kept, as Rogers was suspicious of the Indians.

MAJOR ROBERT ROGERS

From an engraving in the John Ross Robertson Collection,
Toronto Public Library

In the morning, however, they returned with a favourable reply, and the younger warriors of the band agreed to accompany their new friends.   Owing to stormy weather nearly a week passed—the Indians keeping the camp supplied with venison and turkey, for which Rogers paid them liberally—before the party, on November 12, moved forward towards Detroit.

Detroit was at this time under the command of the Sieur de Belêtre, or Bellestre. This officer had been in charge of the post since 1758 and had heard nothing of the surrender of Montreal.   Rogers, to pave the way, sent one of his men in advance with a letter to Belêtre notifying him that the western posts now belonged to King George and informing him that he was approaching with a letter from the Marquis de Vaudreuil and a copy of the capitulation.   Belêtre was irritated ; the French armies had been defeated and he was about to lose his post.   He at first refused to believe the tidings ; and it appears that he endeavoured to rouse the inhabitants and Indians about Detroit to resist the approaching British, for on November 20 several Wyandot sachems met the advancing party and told Rogers that four hundred warriors were in ambush at the entrance to the Detroit river to obstruct his advance. The Wyandots wished to know the truth regarding the conquest of Canada, and on being convinced that it was no fabrication, they took their departure ' in good temper.' On the 23rd Indian messengers, among whom was an Ottawa chief,[1] arrived at the British camp, at the western end of Lake Erie, reporting that Belêtre intended to fight and that he had arrested the officer who bore Rogers's message. Belêtre's chief reason for doubting the truth of Rogers's statement appears to have been that no French officers had accompanied the British contingent from Montreal.

When the troops entered the Detroit river Rogers sent Captain Donald Campbell to the fort with a copy of the capitulation of Montreal and Vaudreuil's letter instructing Belêtre to hand over his fort to the British. These documents were convincing, and Belêtre[2] consented, though with no good grace ; and on

---

[1] In Rogers's journal of this trip no mention is made of Pontiac's name. In *A Concise Account of North America*, published in 1765, with Rogers's name on the title-page, a detailed account of a meeting with Pontiac at the Cuyahoga is given, but this book seems to be of doubtful authenticity. It was, however, accepted by Parkman.

[2] Although Belêtre received Rogers and his men in no friendly

November 29 Rogers formally took possession
of Detroit.   It was an impressive ceremony.
Some seven hundred Indians were assembled
in the vicinity of Fort Detroit, and, ever ready
to take sides with the winning party, appeared
about the stockade painted and plumed in
honour of the occasion.   When the lilies of
France were lowered and the cross of St
George was thrown to the breeze, the barbar-
ous horde uttered wild cries of delight.   A
new and rich people had come to their hunting-grounds, and they had visions of unlimited
presents of clothing, ammunition, and rum.
After the fort was taken over the militia were
called together and disarmed and made to take
the oath of allegiance to the British king.

Captain Campbell was installed in command
of the fort, and Belêtre and the other prisoners
of war were sent to Philadelphia. Two
officers were dispatched with twenty men to
bring the French troops from Forts Miami
and Ouiatanon.   A few soldiers were stationed
at Fort Miami to keep the officers at Detroit
informed of any interesting events in that

spirit, he seems soon to have become reconciled to British rule;
for in 1763 he was appointed to the first Legislative Council of
Canada, and until the time of his death in May 1793 he was a
highly respected citizen of Quebec.

neighbourhood. Provisions being scarce at Detroit, Rogers sent the majority of his force to Niagara ; and on December 10 set out for Michilimackinac with an officer and thirty-seven men. But he was driven back by stormy weather and ice, and forced, for the present year, to give up the attempt to garrison the posts on Lakes Huron and Michigan. Leaving everything in peace at Detroit, Rogers went to Fort Pitt, and for nine months the forts in the country of the Ottawa Confederacy were to be left to their own resources.

Meanwhile the Indians were getting into a state of unrest. The presents, on which they depended so much for existence, were not forthcoming, and rumours of trouble were in the air. Senecas, Shawnees, and Delawares were sending war-belts east and west and north and south. A plot was on foot to seize Pitt, Niagara, and Detroit. Seneca ambassadors had visited the _ Wyandots in the vicinity of Detroit, urging them to fall on the garrison. After an investigation, Captain Campbell reported to Amherst that an Indian rising was imminent, and revealed a plot, originated by the Senecas, which was identical with that afterwards matured in 1763 and attributed to Pontiac's initiative. Campbell

warned the commandants of the other forts of
the danger ; and the Indians, seeing that their
plans were discovered, assumed a peaceful
attitude.

Still, the situation was critical ; and, to
allay the hostility of the natives and gain their
confidence, Amherst dispatched Sir William
Johnson to Detroit with instructions ' to settle
and establish a firm and lasting treaty ' between the British and the Ottawa Confederacy
and other nations inhabiting the Indian territory, to regulate the fur trade at the posts, and
to settle the price of clothes and provisions.
He was likewise to collect information as
exhaustive as possible regarding the Indians,
their manners and customs, and their abodes.
He was to find out whether the French had
any shipping on Lakes Huron, Michigan, and
Superior, what were the best posts for trade,
and the price paid by the French for pelts.
He was also to learn, if possible, how far the
boundaries of Canada extended towards the
Mississippi, and the number of French posts,
settlements, and inhabitants along that river.

Sir William left his home at Fort Johnson
on the Mohawk river early in July 1761.
Scarcely had he begun his journey when he
was warned that it was dangerous to proceed,

as the nations in the west were unfriendly and would surely fall upon his party. But Johnson was confident that his presence among them would put a stop to ' any such wicked design.' As he advanced up Lake Ontario the alarming reports continued. The Senecas, who had already stolen horses from the whites and taken prisoners, had been sending ambassadors abroad, endeavouring to induce the other nations to attack the British. Johnson learned, too, that the Indians were being cheated in trade by British traders; that at several posts they had been roughly handled, very often without cause; that their women were taken from them by violence; and that they were hindered from hunting and fishing on their own grounds near the posts, even what they did catch or kill being taken from them. He heard, too, that Seneca and Ottawa warriors had been murdered by whites near Forts Pitt and Venango. At Niagara he was visited by Seneca chiefs, who complained that one of their warriors had been wounded near by and that four horses had been stolen from them. Johnson evidently believed the story, for he gave them ' two casks of rum, some paint and money to make up their loss,' and they left him well satisfied.

On Lake Erie, stories of the hostility of the
Indians multiplied.   They were ready to re-
volt; even before leaving Niagara, Johnson
had it on good authority that the Indians
'were certainly determined to rise and fall
on the English,' and that 'several thousands
of the Ottawas and other nations' had agreed
to join the dissatisfied member 'of the Six
Nations in this scheme or plot.'   But Johnson kept on his way, confident that he could
allay dissatisfaction and win all the nations to
friendship.

When Sir William reached Detroit on
September 3 he was welcomed by musketry
volleys from the Indians and by cannon from
the fort.   His reputation as the great superintendent of Indian Affairs, the friend of the
red man, had gone before him, and he was
joyously received, and at once given quarters
in the house of the former commandant of
Detroit, Belêtre.   On the day following his
arrival the Wyandots and other Indians,
with their priest, Father Pierre Potier (called
Pottie by Johnson), waited on him.   He
treated them royally, and gave them pipes and
tobacco and a barbecue of a large ox roasted
whole.   He found the French inhabitants
most friendly, especially Pierre Chesne, better

known as La Butte, the interpreter of the
Wyandots, and St Martin, the interpreter of
the Ottawas. The ladies of the settlement
called on him, and were regaled ' with cakes,
wine and cordial.' He was hospitably enter-
tained by the officers and settlers, and in return gave several balls, at which, it appears,
he danced with ' Mademoiselle Curie—a fine
girl.' This vivacious lady evidently made
an impression on the susceptible Irishman ;
for after the second ball—' there never was
so brilliant an affair ' at Detroit before—he
records in his private diary : ' Promised to
write Mademoiselle Curie my sentiments.'

While at Niagara on his journey westward
Johnson had been joined by Major Henry
Gladwyn, to whom Amherst had assigned the
duty of garrisoning the western forts and
taking over in person the command of Fort
Detroit. Gladwyn had left Niagara a day or
two in advance of Johnson, but on the way
to his new command he had been seized with
severe fever and ague and totally incapacitated
for duty. On Johnson fell the task of making
arrangements for the still unoccupied posts.
He did the work with his customary prompti-
tude and thoroughness, and by September 10
had dispatched men of Gage's Light Infantry

and of the Royal Americans from Detroit for Michilimackinac, Green Bay, and St Joseph.

The chiefs of the various tribes had flocked to Detroit to confer with Sir William. He won them all by his honeyed words and liberal distribution of presents ; he was told that his ' presents had made the sun and sky bright and clear, the earth smooth and level, the roads all pleasant ' ; and they begged that he ' would continue in the same friendly disposition towards them and they would be a happy people.' His work completed, Johnson set out, September 19, on his homeward journey, leaving behind him the promise of peace in the Indian territory.[1]

For the time being Johnson's visit to Detroit had a salutary effect, and the year 1761 terminated with only slight signs of unrest among the Indians ; but in the spring of 1762 the air was again heavy with threatening storm. The Indians of the Ohio valley were once more sending out their war-belts and bloody hatchets. In several instances Englishmen were murdered and scalped and horses were stolen. The Shawnees and Dela-

---

[1] It is remarkable that Johnson in his private diary or in his official correspondence makes no mention of Pontiac. The Ottawa chief apparently played no conspicuous part in the plots of 1761 and 1762.

wares held British prisoners whom they refused to surrender. By Amherst's orders presents were withheld. Until they surrendered all prisoners and showed a proper spirit towards the British he would suppress all gifts, in the belief that ' a due observance of this alone will soon produce more than can ever be expected from bribing them.' The reply of the Shawnees and Delawares to his orders was stealing horses and terrorizing traders. Sir William Johnson and his assistant in office, George Croghan, warned Amherst of the danger he was running in rousing the hatred of the savages. Croghan in a letter to Bouquet said : ' I do not approve of General Amherst's plan of distressing them too much, as in my opinion they will not consider consequences if too much distressed, tho' Sir Jeffery thinks they will.' Although warnings were pouring in upon him, Amherst was of the opinion that there was ' no necessity for any more at the several posts than are just enough to keep up the communication, there being nothing to fear from the Indians in our present circumstances.' To Sir William Johnson he wrote that it was ' not in the power of the Indians to effect anything of consequence.'

In the spring of 1763 the war-cloud was about to burst ; but in remote New York the commander-in-chief failed to grasp the situation, and turned a deaf ear to those who warned him that an Indian war with all its horrors was inevitable.   These vague rumours, as Amherst regarded them, of an imminent general rising of the western tribes, took more definite form as the spring advanced. Towards the end of March Lieutenant Edward Jenkins, the commandant of Fort Ouiatanon, learned that the French traders had been telling the Indians that the British would 'all be prisoners in a short time.'   But what caused most alarm was information from Fort Miami of a plot for the capture of the forts and the slaughter of the garrisons. A war-belt was received by the Indians residing near the fort, and with it came the request that they should hold themselves in readiness to attack the British. Robert Holmes, the commandant of Fort Miami, managed to secure the 'bloody belt' and sent it to Gladwyn,[1] who in turn sent it to Amherst.

News had now reached the Ohio tribes of

[1] Gladwyn's illness in 1761 proved so severe that he had to take a journey to England to recuperate ; but he was back in Detroit as commandant in August 1762.

the Treaty of Paris, but the terms of this treaty
had only increased their unrest.   On April 30,
1763, Croghan wrote to Amherst that the
Indians were ' uneasy since so much of North
America was ceded to Great Britain,' holding that the British had no right in their
country.   ' The Peace,' added Croghan, ' and
hearing so much of this country being given
up has thrown them into confusion and prevented them bringing in their prisoners this
spring as they promised.'   Amherst's reply
was : ' Whatever idle notions they may entertain in regard to the cessions made by the
French crown can be of very little consequence.'   On April 20 Gladwyn, though slow
to see danger, wrote to Amherst : ' They [the
Indians] say we mean to make Slaves of them
by Taking so many posts in the country,
and that they had better attempt Something
now to Recover their liberty than wait till we
are better established.'   Even when word that
the Indians were actually on the war-path
reached Amherst, he still refused to believe it
a serious matter, and delayed making preparations to meet the situation.   It was, according
to him, a 'rash attempt of that turbulent tribe
the Senecas '; and, again, he was ' persuaded
this alarm will end in nothing more than a

rash attempt of what the Senecas have been threatening.' Eight British forts in the west were captured and the frontiers of the colonies bathed in blood before he realized that 'the affair of the Indians was more general than they apprehended.'

The Indians were only waiting for a sudden, bold blow at some one of the British posts, and on the instant they would be on the war-path from the shores of Lake Superior to the borders of the southernmost colonies of Great Britain. The blow was soon to be struck. Pontiac's war-belts had been sent broadcast, and the nations who recognized him as over-chief were ready to follow him to the slaughter. Detroit was the strongest position to the west of Niagara ; it contained an abundance of stores, and would be a rich prize. As Pontiac yearly visited this place during the trading season, he knew the locality well and was familiar with the settlers, the majority of whom were far from being friendly to the British. Against Detroit he would lead the warriors, under the pretence of winning back the country for the French.

In the spring of 1763, instead of going direct to his usual camping-place, an island in Lake St Clair, Pontiac pitched his wig-

wam on the bank of the river Ecorces, ten
miles south of Detroit, and here awaited the
tribes whom he had summoned to a council to
be held ' on the 15th of the moon '—the 27th
of April.   And at the appointed time nearly
five hundred warriors — Ottawas, Potawatomis, Chippewas, and Wyandots—with their
squaws and papooses, had gathered at the
meeting - place, petty tribal jealousies and
differences being laid aside in their common
hatred of ' the dogs dressed in red,' the British
soldiers.

When the council assembled Pontiac addressed them with fiery words.   The Ottawa
chief was at this time about fifty years old.
He was a man of average height, of darker
hue than is usual among Indians, lithe as a
panther, his muscles hardened by forest life
and years of warfare against Indian enemies
and the British.   Like the rush of a mountain
torrent the words fell from his lips.   His
speech was one stream of denunciation of
the British.   In trade they had cheated the
Indians, robbing them of their furs, over-
charging them for the necessaries of life,
and heaping insults and blows upon the red
men, who from the French had known only
kindness.   The time had come to strike.   As

he spoke he flashed a red and purple wampum
belt before the gaze of the excited braves.
This, he declared, he had received from their
father the king of France, who commanded
his red children to fight the British.   Holding out the belt, he recounted with wild words
and vehement gestures the victories gained
in the past by the Indians over the British,
and as he spoke the blood of his listeners
pulsed through their veins with battle ardour.
To their hatred and sense of being wronged
he had appealed, and he saw that every warrior
present was with him; but his strongest
appeal was to their superstition.   In spite of
the fact that French missionaries had been
among them for a century, they were still
pagan, and it was essential to the success of
his project that they should believe that the
Master of Life favoured their cause.   He told
them the story of a Wolf (Delaware) Indian
who had journeyed to heaven and talked with
the Master of Life, receiving instructions to
tell all the Indians that they were to ' drive
out ' and ' make war upon ' the ' dogs clothed
in red who will do you nothing but harm.'
When he had finished, such chiefs as Ninevois
of the Chippewas and Takay of the Wyandots
—' the bad Hurons,' as the writer of the

' Pontiac Manuscript ' describes them to distinguish them from Father Potier's flock—spoke in similar terms.   Every warrior present shouted his readiness to go to war, and before the council broke up it was agreed that in four days Pontiac ' should go to the fort with his young men for a peace dance ' in order to get information regarding the strength of the place.   The blow must be struck before the spring boats arrived from the Niagara with supplies and additional troops.   The council at an end, the different tribes scattered to their several summer villages, seemingly peaceful Indians who had gathered together for trade.

CHAPTER IV

THE SIEGE OF DETROIT

AT the time of the Pontiac outbreak there were in the vicinity of Fort Detroit between one thousand and two thousand white inhabitants. Yet the place was little more than a wilderness post. The settlers were cut off from civilization and learned news of the great world outside only in the spring, when the traders' boats came with supplies. They were out of touch with Montreal and Quebec, and it was difficult for them to realize that they were subjects of the hated king of England. They had not lost their confidence that the armies of France would yet be victorious and sweep the British from the Great Lakes, and in this opinion they were strengthened by traders from the Mississippi, who came among them. But the change of rulers had made little difference in their lives. The majority of them were employed by traders, and the better class contentedly cultivated their narrow farms and traded with the Indians who periodically visited them.

The settlement was widely scattered, extending along the east shore of the Detroit river for about eight miles from Lake St Clair, and along the west shore for about six miles, four above and two below the fort. On either side of the river the fertile fields and the long row of whitewashed, low-built houses, with their gardens and orchards of apple and pear trees, fenced about with rounded pickets, presented a picture of peace and plenty. The summers of the inhabitants were enlivened by the visits of the Indians and the traders; and in winter they light-heartedly whiled away the tedious hours with gossip and dance and feast, like the habitants along the Richelieu and the St Lawrence.

The militia of the settlement, as we have seen, had been deprived of their arms at the taking over of Detroit by Robert Rogers; and for the most part the settlers maintained a stolid attitude towards their conquerors, from whom they suffered no hardship and whose rule was not galling. The British had nothing to fear from them. But the Indians were a force to be reckoned with. There were three Indian villages in the vicinity—the Wyandot,

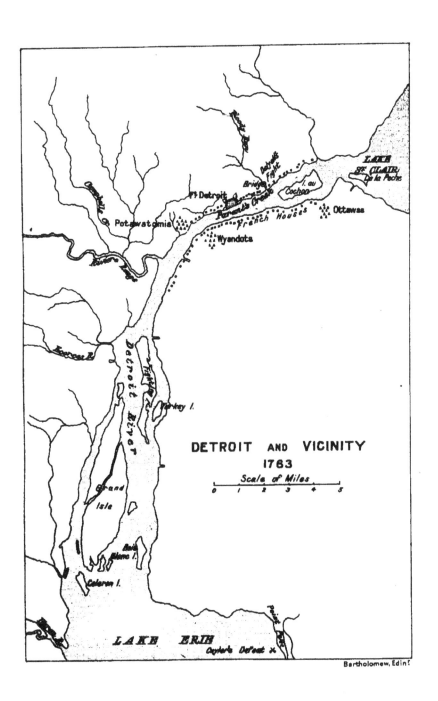

DETROIT AND VICINITY
1763

Scale of Miles

0   1   2   3   4   5

Bartholomew, Edinʳ

on the east side of the river, opposite the fort ; the Ottawa, five miles above, opposite Ile au Cochon (Belle Isle) ; and the Potawatomi, about two miles below the fort on the west shore.   The Ottawas here could muster 200 warriors, the Potawatomis about 150, and the Wyandots 250, while near at hand were the Chippewas, 320 strong.   Pontiac, although head chief of the Ottawas, did not live in the village, but had his wigwam on Ile à la Pêche, at the outlet of Lake St Clair, a spot where whitefish abounded.   Here he dwelt with his squaws and papooses, not in ' grandeur,' but in squalid savagery.   Between the Indians and the French there existed a most friendly relationship ; many of the habitants, indeed, having Indian wives.

Near the centre of the settlement, on the west bank of the river, about twenty miles from Lake Erie, stood Fort Detroit, a miniature town.   It was in the form of a parallelogram and was surrounded by a palisade twenty-five feet high.   According to a letter of an officer, the walls had an extent of over one thousand paces.   At each corner was a bastion and over each gate a blockhouse. Within the walls were about one hundred houses, the little Catholic church of Ste Anne's, a council - house, officers' quarters, and a range of barracks. Save for one or two exceptions the buildings were of wood, thatched with bark or straw, and stood close together. The streets were exceedingly narrow; but immediately within the palisade a wide road extended round the entire village. The spiritual welfare of the French and Indian Catholics in the garrison was looked after by Father Potier, a Jesuit, whose mission was in the Wyandot village, and by Father Bocquet, a Récollet, who lived within the fort. Major Henry Gladwyn was in command. He had a hundred and twenty soldiers, and two armed schooners, the *Gladwyn* and the *Beaver*, were in the river near by.

On the first day of May 1763, Pontiac came to the main gate of the fort asking to be allowed to enter, as he and the warriors with him, forty in all, desired to show their love for the British by dancing the calumet or peace dance. Gladwyn had not the slightest suspicion of evil intent, and readily admitted them. The savages selected a spot in front of the officers' houses, and thirty of them went through their grotesque movements, shouting and dancing to the music of the Indian drum, and all the while waving their calumets in token of friend-

ship.   While the dancers were thus engaged,
the remaining ten of the party were busily
employed in surveying the fort—noting the
number of men and the strength of the
palisades.   The dance lasted about an hour.
Presents were then distributed to the Indians,
and all took their departure.

Pontiac now summoned the Indians about
Detroit to another council.   On this occasion the chiefs and warriors assembled in
the council-house in the Potawatomi village
south of the fort.   When all were gathered
together Pontiac rose and, as at the council
at the river Ecorces, in a torrent of words
and with vehement gestures, denounced the
British.   He declared that under the new
occupancy of the forts in the Indian country
the red men were neglected and their wants
were no longer supplied as they had been in
the days of the French ; that exorbitant prices
were charged by the traders for goods ; that
when the Indians were departing for their
winter camps to hunt for furs they were no
longer able to obtain ammunition and clothing
on credit ; and, finally, that the British desired
the death of the Indians, and it was therefore necessary as an act of self-preservation
to destroy them.   He once more displayed

the war-belt that he pretended to have received from the king of France. This belt told him to strike in his own interest and in the interest of the French. He closed his speech by saying that he had sent belts to the Chippewas of Saginaw and the Ottawas of Michilimackinac and of the river La Tranche (the Thames). Seeing that his words were greeted with grunts and shouts of approval and that the assembled warriors were with him to a man, Pontiac revealed a plan he had formed to seize the fort and slaughter the garrison. He and some fifty chiefs and warriors would wait on Gladwyn on the pretence of discussing matters of importance. Each one would carry beneath his blanket a gun, with the barrel cut short to permit of concealment. Warriors and even women were to enter the fort as if on a friendly visit and take up positions of advantage in the streets, in readiness to strike with tomahawks, knives, and guns, all which they were to have concealed beneath their blankets. At the council Pontiac was to address Gladwyn and, in pretended friendship, hand him a wampum belt. If it were wise to strike, he would on presenting the belt hold its reverse side towards Gladwyn. This was to be the signal for attack.   Instantly blankets were to be thrown aside and the officers were to be shot down.   At the sound of firing in the council-room the Indians in the streets were to fall on the garrison and every British soldier was to be slain, care being taken that no Frenchman suffered.   The plan, by its treachery, and by its possibilities of slaughter and plunder, appealed to the savages; and they dispersed to make preparations for the morning of the 7th, the day chosen for carrying out the murderous scheme.

The plot was difficult to conceal.   The aid of French blacksmiths had to be sought to shorten the guns.   Moreover, the British garrison had some friends among the Indians. Scarcely had the plot been matured when it was discussed among the French, and on the day before the intended massacre it was revealed to Gladwyn.   His informant is not certainly known.   A Chippewa maiden, an old squaw, several Frenchmen, and an Ottawa named Mahiganne have been mentioned.   It is possible that Gladwyn had it from a number of sources, but most likely from Mahiganne. The ' Pontiac Manuscript,' probably the work of Robert Navarre, the keeper of the notarial records of the settlement, distinctly states that

Mahiganne revealed the details of the plot with the request that Gladwyn should not divulge his name ; for, should Pontiac learn, the informer would surely be put to death. This would account for the fact that Gladwyn, even in his report of the affair to Amherst, gives no hint as to the person who told him.

Gladwyn at once made preparations to receive Pontiac and his chiefs. On the night of the 6th instructions were given to the soldiers and the traders within the fort to make preparations to resist an attack, and the guards were doubled. As the sentries peered out into the darkness occasional yells and whoops and the beating of drums reached their ears, telling of the war-dance that was being performed in the Indian villages to hearten the warriors for the slaughter.

Gladwyn determined to act boldly. On the morning of the 7th all the traders' stores were closed and every man capable of bearing weapons was under arms ; but the gates were left open as usual, and shortly after daylight Indians and squaws by twos and threes began to gather in the fort as if to trade. At ten in the morning a line of chiefs with Pontiac at their head filed along the road leading to the river gate. All were painted and plumed

and each one was wrapped in a brightly
coloured blanket. When they entered the
fort they were astonished to see the warlike
preparations, but stoically concealed their surprise. Arrived in the council-chamber, the
chiefs noticed the sentinels standing at arms,
the commandant and his officers seated, their
faces stern and set, pistols in their belts and
swords by their sides. So perturbed were
the chiefs by all this warlike display that it
was some time before they would take their
seats on the mats prepared for them. At
length they recovered their composure, and
Pontiac broke the silence by asking why so
many of the young men were standing in the
streets with their guns. Answer was made
through the interpreter La Butte that it was
for exercise and discipline. Pontiac then
addressed Gladwyn, vehemently protesting
friendship. All the time he was speaking
Gladwyn bent on him a scrutinizing gaze, and
as the chief was about to present the wampum belt, a signal was given and the drums
crashed out a charge. Every doubt was removed from Pontiac's mind—his plot was discovered. His nervous hand lowered the belt ;
but he recovered himself immediately and
presented it in the ordinary way. Gladwyn

replied to his speech sternly, but kindly, saying that he would have the protection and friendship of the British so long as he merited it. A few presents were then distributed among the Indians, and the council ended. The chiefs, with their blankets still tightly wrapped about them, filed out of the council-room and scattered to their villages, followed by the disappointed rabble of fully three hundred Indians, who had assembled in the fort.

On the morrow, Pontiac, accompanied by three chiefs, again appeared at the fort, bringing with him a pipe of peace. When this had been smoked by the officers and chiefs, he presented it to Captain Campbell, as a further mark of friendship. The next day he was once more at the gates seeking entrance. But he found them closed: Gladwyn felt that the time had come to take no chances. This morning a rabble of Potawatomis, Ottawas, Wyandots, and Chippewas thronged the common just out of musket range. On Pontiac's request for a conference with Gladwyn he was sternly told that he might enter alone. The answer angered him, and he strode back to his followers. Now, with yells and war-whoops, parties of the savages bounded away on a murderous mission. Half a mile behind the fort an English woman, Mrs Turnbull, and her two sons cultivated a small farm. All three were straightway slain. A party of Ottawas leapt into their canoes and paddled swiftly to Ile au Cochon, where lived a former sergeant, James Fisher. Fisher was seized, killed, and scalped, his young wife brutally murdered, and their two little children carried into captivity. On this same day news was brought to the fort that Sir Robert Davers and Captain Robertson had been murdered three days before on Lake St Clair by Chippewas who were on their way from Saginaw to join Pontiac's forces. Thus began the Pontiac War in the vicinity of Detroit. For several months the garrison was to know little rest.

That night at the Ottawa village arose the hideous din of the war-dance, and while the warriors worked themselves into a frenzy the squaws were busy breaking camp. Before daylight the village was moved to the opposite side of the river, and the wigwams were pitched near the mouth of Parent's Creek, about a mile and a half above the fort. On the morning of the 10th the siege began in earnest. Shortly after daybreak the yells of a horde of savages could be heard north and

south and west.   But few of the enemy could
be seen, as they had excellent shelter behind
barns, outhouses, and fences.   For six hours
they kept up a continuous fire on the garrison, but wounded only five men.   The fort
vigorously returned the fire, and none of the
enemy dared attempt to rush the palisades.
A cluster of buildings in the rear sheltered a
particularly ferocious set of savages.   A three-
pounder—the only effective artillery in the
fort—was trained on this position ;   spikes
were bound together with wire, heated red-
hot, and fired at the buildings.   These were
soon a mass of flames, and the savages concealed behind them fled for their lives.

Presently the Indians grew tired of this
useless warfare and withdrew to their villages.
Gladwyn, thinking that he might bring Pontiac
to terms, sent La Butte to ask the cause of the
attack and to say that the British were ready
to redress any wrongs from which the Indians
might be suffering.   La Butte was accompanied by Jean Baptiste Chapoton, a captain
of the militia and a man of some importance
in the fort, and Jacques Godfroy, a trader
and likewise an officer of militia.   It may be
noted that Godfroy's wife was the daughter
of a Miami chief.   The ambassadors were re-

ceived in a friendly manner by Pontiac, who
seemed ready to cease hostilities.   La Butte
returned to the fort with some of the chiefs
to report progress; but when he went again
to Pontiac he found that the Ottawa chief had
made no definite promise.   It seems probable,
judging from their later actions, that Chapoton
and Godfroy had betrayed Gladwyn and urged
Pontiac to force the British out of the country.
Pontiac now requested that Captain Donald
Campbell, who had been in charge of Detroit
before Gladwyn took over the command,
should come to his village to discuss terms.
Campbell was confident that he could pacify
the Indians, and, accompanied by Lieutenant
George M'Dougall, he set out along the river
road for the Ottawas' encampment at Parent's
Creek.   As the two officers crossed the bridge
at the mouth of the creek, they were met by
a savage crowd—men, women, and children
—armed with sticks and clubs.   The mob
rushed at them with yells and threatening
gestures, and were about to fall on the officers
when Pontiac appeared and restored order.
A council was held, but as Campbell could
get no satisfaction he suggested returning to
the fort.   Thereupon Pontiac remarked: 'My
father will sleep to-night in the lodges of his

red children.' Campbell and M'Dougall were
given good quarters in the house of Jean
Baptiste Meloche. For nearly two months
they were to be kept close prisoners.

So far only part of the Wyandots had
joined Pontiac : Father Potier had been trying to keep his flock neutral. But on the 11th
Pontiac crossed to the Wyandot village, and
threatened it with destruction if the warriors
did not take up the tomahawk. On this com-
pulsion they consented, no doubt glad of an
excuse to be rid of the discipline of their
priest.

Another attack on the fort was made, this
time by about six hundred Indians ; but it
was as futile as the one of the earlier day.
Pontiac now tried negotiation. He summoned Gladwyn to surrender, promising that
the British should be allowed to depart un-
molested on their vessels. The officers, knowing that their communications with the east
were cut, that food was scarce, that a vigorous
assault could not fail to carry the fort, urged
Gladwyn to accept the offer, but he sternly
refused. He would not abandon Detroit
while one pound of food and one pound of
powder were left in the fort. Moreover, the
treacherous conduct of Pontiac convinced him

that the troops and traders as they left the fort would be plundered and slaughtered.   He rejected Pontiac's demands, and advised him to disperse his people and save his ammunition for hunting.

At this critical moment Detroit was undoubtedly saved by a French Canadian.   But for Jacques Bâby, the grim spectre Starvation would have stalked through the little fortress. Bâby was a prosperous trader and merchant who, with his wife Susanne Reaume, lived on the east shore of the river, almost opposite the fort.   He had a farm of one thousand acres, two hundred of which were under cultivation.   His trading establishment was a low-built log structure eighty feet long by twenty wide.   He owned thirty slaves— twenty men and ten women.   He seems to have treated them kindly; at any rate, they loyally did his will.   Bâby agreed to get provisions into the fort by stealth ; and on a dark night, about a week after the siege commenced, Gladwyn had a lantern displayed on a plank fixed at the water's edge.   Bâby had six canoes in readiness ;   in each were stowed two quarters of beef, three hogs, and six bags of meal.   All night long these canoes plied across the half-mile stretch of water and by

daylight sufficient food to last the garrison
for several weeks had been delivered.

From day to day the Indians kept up a
desultory firing, while Gladwyn took precau-
tions against a long siege.   Food was taken
from the houses of the inhabitants and placed
in a common storehouse.   Timber was torn
from the walks and used in the construction
of portable bastions, which were erected outside the fort.   There being danger that the
roofs of the houses would be ignited by means
of fire-arrows, the French inhabitants of the
fort were made to draw water and store it in
vessels at convenient points.   Houses, fences,
and orchards in the neighbourhood were destroyed and levelled, so that skulking warriors
could not find shelter.   The front of the fort
was comparatively safe from attack, for the
schooners guarded the river gate, and the Indians had a wholesome dread of these floating
fortresses.

About the middle of the month the *Gladwyn*
sailed down the Detroit to meet a convoy
that was expected with provisions and
ammunition from Fort Schlosser.   At the
entrance to Lake Erie, as the vessel lay becalmed in the river, she was suddenly beset
by a swarm of savages in canoes;   and

Pontiac's prisoner, Captain Campbell, appeared in the foremost canoe, the savages thinking that the British would not fire on them for fear of killing him. Happily, a breeze sprang up and the schooner escaped to the open lake. There was no sign of the convoy; and the *Gladwyn* sailed for the Niagara, to carry to the officers there tidings of the Indian rising in the west.

On May 30 the watchful sentries at Detroit saw a line of bateaux flying the British flag rounding a point on the east shore of the river. This was the expected convoy from Fort Schlosser, and the cannon boomed forth a welcome. But the rejoicings of the garrison were soon stilled. Instead of British cheers, wild war-whoops resounded from the bateaux. The Indians had captured the convoy and were forcing their captives to row. In the foremost boat were four soldiers and three savages. Nearing the fortress one of the soldiers conceived the daring plan of overpowering the Indian guard and escaping to the *Beaver*, which lay anchored in front of the fort. Seizing the nearest savage he attempted to throw him into the river; but the Indian succeeded in stabbing him, and both fell overboard and were drowned. The other savages, dreading capture, leapt out of the boat and swam ashore. The bateau with the three soldiers in it reached the *Beaver*, and the provisions and ammunition it contained were taken to the fort. The Indians in the remaining bateaux, warned by the fate of the leading vessel, landed on the east shore ; and, marching their prisoners overland past the fort, they took them across the river to Pontiac's camp, where most of them were put to death with fiendish cruelty.

The soldiers who escaped to the *Beaver* told the story of the ill-fated convoy. On May 13 Lieutenant Abraham Cuyler, totally ignorant of the outbreak of hostilities at Detroit, had left Fort Schlosser with ninety-six men in ten bateaux. They had journeyed in leisurely fashion along the northern shore of Lake Erie, and by the 28th had reached Point Pelée, about thirty miles from the Detroit river. Here a landing was made, and while tents were being pitched a band of painted savages suddenly darted out of the forest and attacked a man and a boy who were gathering wood. The man escaped, but the boy was tomahawked and scalped. Cuyler drew up his men in front of the boats, and a sharp musketry fire followed between the

Indians, who were sheltered by a thick wood, and the white men on the exposed shore. The raiders were Wyandots from Detroit, the most courageous and intelligent savages in the region. Seeing that Cuyler's men were panic-stricken, they broke from their cover, with unusual boldness for Indians, and made a mad charge. The soldiers, completely unnerved by the savage yells and hurtling tomahawks, threw down their arms and dashed in confusion to the boats. Five they succeeded in pushing off, and into these they tumbled without weapons of defence. Cuyler himself was left behind wounded ; but he waded out, and was taken aboard under a brisk fire from the shore. The Indians then launched two of the abandoned boats, rushed in pursuit of the fleeing soldiers, speedily captured three of the boats, and brought them ashore in triumph. The two others, in one of which was Cuyler, hoisted sail and escaped. The Indians, as we have seen, brought the captured boats and their prisoners to Detroit. Cuyler had directed his course to Sandusky, but finding the blockhouse there burnt to the ground, he had rowed eastward to Presqu'isle, and then hastened to Niagara to report the disaster.

The siege of Detroit went on.   Towards the middle of June, Jacques Bâby brought word to the commandant that the *Gladwyn* was returning from the Niagara with supplies and men, and that the Indians were making preparations to capture her.   A few miles below Detroit lay Fighting Island ; between it and the east shore, Turkey Island.   Here the savages had erected a breastwork, so carefully concealed that it would be difficult even for the keenest eyes to detect its presence.   The vessel would have to pass within easy range of this barricade; and it was the plan of the Indians to dart out in their canoes as the schooner worked up-stream, seize her, and slay her crew.   On learning this news Gladwyn ordered cannon to be fired to notify the captain that the fort still held out, and sent a messenger to meet the vessel with word of the plot.   It happened that the *Gladwyn* was well manned and prepared for battle.   On board was Cuyler with twenty-two survivors of the ill-starred convoy, besides twenty-eight men of Captain Hopkins's company.   To deceive the Indians as to the number of men, all the crew and soldiers, save ten or twelve, were concealed in the hold ; to invite attack, the vessel advanced boldly up-stream, and at

nightfall cast anchor in the narrow channel
in front of Turkey Island. About midnight
the Indians stealthily boarded their canoes
and cautiously, but confidently, swept towards
her with muffled paddles. The *Gladwyn* was
ready for them. Not a sound broke the
silence of the night as the Indians approached
the schooner; when suddenly the clang of
a hammer against the mast echoed over
the calm waters, the signal to the soldiers
in the hold. The Indians were almost on
their prey; but before they had time to utter
the war-whoop, the soldiers had come up and
had attacked the savages with bullets and
cannon shot. Shrieks of death arose amid
the din of the firing and the splash of swimmers
hurriedly making for the shore from the sinking canoes. In a moment fourteen Indians
were killed and as many more wounded. From
behind the barricade the survivors began a
harmless musketry fire against the schooner,
which simply weighed anchor and drifted
down-stream to safety. A day or two later
she cleared Turkey Island and reached the
fort, pouring a shattering broadside into the
Wyandot village as she passed it. Besides
the troops, the *Gladwyn* had on board a pre-
cious cargo of a hundred and fifty barrels of

provisions and some ammunition. She had not run the blockade unscathed, for in passing Turkey Island one sergeant and four men had been wounded. There was rejoicing in the fort when the reinforcement marched in. This additional strength in men and provisions, it was expected, would enable the garrison to hold out for at least another month, within which time soldiers would arrive in sufficient force to drive the Indians away.

In the meantime Pontiac was becoming alarmed. He had expected an easy victory, and was not prepared for a protracted siege. He had drawn on the French settlers for supplies ; his warriors had slain cattle and taken provisions without the consent of the owners. Leaders in the settlement now waited on Pontiac, making complaint. He professed to be fighting for French rule, and expressed sorrow at the action of his young men, promising that in future the French should be paid. Acting, no doubt, on the suggestion of some of his French allies, he made a list of the inhabitants, drew on each for a definite quantity of supplies, and had these deposited at Meloche's house near his camp on Parent's Creek. A commissary was appointed to distribute the provisions as required. In payment he issued letters of credit, signed with his totem, the otter. It is said that all of them were afterwards redeemed ; but this is almost past belief in the face of what actually happened.

From the beginning of the siege Pontiac had hoped that the French traders and settlers would join him to force the surrender of the fort. The arrival of the reinforcement under Cuyler made him despair of winning without their assistance, and early in July he sent his Indians to the leading inhabitants along the river, ordering them to a council, at which he hoped by persuasion or threats to make them take up arms. This council was attended by such settlers as Robert Navarre, Zacharie Sicotte, Louis Campau, Antoine Cuillerier, François Meloche, all men of standing and influence. In his address to them Pontiac declared : ' If you are French, accept this war-belt for yourselves, or your young men, and join us ; if you are English, we declare war upon you.'

The *Gladwyn* had brought news of the Peace of Paris between France and England. Many of the settlers had been hoping that success would crown the French arms in Europe and that Canada would be restored. Some of

those at the council said that these articles
of peace were a mere ruse on the part of
Gladwyn to gain time.   Robert Navarre, who
had published the articles of peace to the
French and Indians, and several others were
friendly to the British, but the majority of,
those present were unfriendly.   Sicotte told
Pontiac that, while the heads of families could
not take up arms, there were three hundred
young men about Detroit who would willingly
join him.   These words were probably intended to humour the chief ; but there were
those who took the belt and commenced recruiting among their fellows.   The settlers
who joined Pontiac were nearly all half-
breeds or men mated with Indian wives.
Others, such as Pierre Reaume and Louis
Campau, believing their lives to be in danger
on account of their loyalty to the new rulers,
sought shelter in the fort.

By July 4 the Indians, under the direction
of French allies, had strongly entrenched
themselves and had begun a vigorous attack.
But a force of about sixty men marched out
from the fort and drove them from the
position.   In the retreat two Indians were
killed, and one of the pursuing soldiers, who
had been a prisoner among the Indians and

had learned the ways of savage warfare, scalped one of the fallen braves. The victim proved to be a nephew of the chief of the Saginaw Chippewas, who now claimed life for life, and demanded that Captain Campbell should be given up to him. According to the ' Pontiac Manuscript ' Pontiac acquiesced, and the Saginaw chief killed Campbell ' with a blow of his tomahawk, and after cast him into the river.' Campbell's fellow-prisoner M'Dougall, along with two others, had escaped to the fort some days before.

The investment continued, although the attacks became less frequent. The schooners manœuvring in the river poured broadsides into the Indian villages, battering down the flimsy wigwams. Pontiac moved his camp from the mouth of Parent's Creek to a position nearer Lake St Clair, out of range of their guns, and turned his thoughts to contrive some means of destroying the troublesome vessels. He had learned from the French of the attempt with fire-ships against the British fleet at Quebec, and made trial of a simi- lar artifice. Bateaux were joined together, loaded with inflammable material, ignited, and sent on their mission; but these ' fire- ships ' floated harmlessly past the schooners and burnt themselves out.   Then for a week the Indians worked on the construction of a gigantic fire-raft, but nothing came of this ambitious scheme.

It soon appeared that Pontiac was beginning to lose his hold on the Indians.   About the middle of July ambassadors from the Wyandots and Potawatomis came to the fort with an offer of peace, protesting, after the Indian manner, love and friendship for the British. After much parleying they surrendered their prisoners and plunder ; but, soon after, a temptation irresistible to their treacherous natures offered itself, and they were again on the war-path.

Amherst at New York had at last been aroused to the danger ; and Captain James Dalyell had set out from Fort Schlosser with twenty-two barges, carrying nearly three hundred men, with cannon and supplies, for the relief of Detroit.   The expedition skirted the southern shore of Lake Erie until it reached Sandusky.   The Wyandot villages here were found deserted.   After destroying them Dalyell shaped his course for the Detroit river. Fortune favoured the expedition.   Pontiac was either ignorant of its approach or unable to mature a plan to check its advance.

Through the darkness and fog of the night of July 28 the barges cautiously crept up-stream, and when the morning sun of the 29th lifted the mists from the river they were in full view of the fort. Relief at last ! The weary watching of months was soon to end. The band of the fort was assembled, and the martial airs of England floated on the morning breeze. Now it was that the Wyandots and Potawatomis, although so lately swearing friendship to the British, thought the opportunity too good to be lost. In passing their villages the barges were assailed by a musketry fire, which killed two and wounded thirteen of Dalyell's men. But the soldiers, with muskets and swivels, replied to the attack, and put the Indians to flight. Then the barges drew up before the fort to the welcome of the anxious watchers of Detroit.

The reinforcement was composed of men of the 55th and 8th regiments, and of twenty Rangers under Major Robert Rogers. Like their commander, Dalyell, many of them were experienced in Indian fighting and were eager to be at Pontiac and his warriors. Dalyell thought that Pontiac might be taken by surprise, and urged on Gladwyn the advisability of an immediate advance. To this Gladwyn was averse; but Dalyell was insistent, and won his point. By the following night all was in readiness. At two o'clock in the morning of the 31st the river gate was thrown open and about two hundred and fifty men filed out.

Heavy clouds hid both moon and stars, and the air was oppressively hot. The soldiers marched along the dusty road, guided by Bâby and St Martin, who had volunteered for the work. Not a sound save their own dull tramp broke the silence. On their right gleamed the calm river, and keeping pace with them were two large bateaux armed with swivels. Presently, as the troops passed the farm-houses, drowsy watch-dogs caught the sound of marching feet and barked furiously. Pontiac's camp, however, was still far away; this barking would not alarm the Indians. But the soldiers did not know that they had been betrayed by a spy of Pontiac's within the fort, nor did they suspect that snake-like eyes were even then watching their advance.

At length Parent's Creek was reached, where a narrow wooden bridge spanned the stream a few yards from its mouth. The advance-guard were half-way over the bridge, and the main body crowding after them, when, from a black ridge in front, the crackle of musketry arose, and half the advance-guard fell. The narrow stream ran red with their blood, and ever after this night it was known as Bloody Run. On the high ground to the north of the creek a barricade of cordwood had been erected, and behind this and behind barns and houses and fences, and in the corn-fields and orchards, Indians were firing and yelling like demons. The troops recoiled, but Dalyell rallied them; again they crowded to the bridge. There was another volley and another pause. With reckless bravery the soldiers pressed across the narrow way and rushed to the spot where the musket-flashes were seen. They won the height, but not an Indian was there. The musket-flashes con-tinued and war-whoops sounded from new shelters. The bateaux drew up alongside the bridge, and the dead and wounded were taken on board to be carried to the fort. It was useless to attempt to drive the shifty savages from their lairs, and so the retreat was sounded. Captain Grant, in charge of the rear company, led his men back across the bridge while Dalyell covered the retreat; and now the fight took on a new aspect.

As the soldiers retreated along the road leading to the fort, a destructive fire poured upon them from houses and barns, from behind fences, and from a newly dug cellar. With the river on their left, and with the enemy before and behind as well as on their right, they were in danger of being annihilated. Grant ordered his men to fix bayonets: a dash was made where the savages were thickest, and they were scattered. As the fire was renewed panic seized the troops. But Dalyell came up from the rear, and with shouts and threats and flat of sword restored order. Day was breaking; but a thick fog hung over the scene, under cover of which the Indians continued the attack. The house of Jacques Campau, a trader, sheltered a number of Indians who were doing most destructive work. Rogers and a party of his Rangers attacked the house, and, pounding in the doors, drove out their assailants. From Campau's house Rogers covered the retreat of Grant's company, but was himself in turn besieged. By this time the armed bateaux, which had borne the dead and wounded to the fort, had returned, and, opening fire with their swivels on the Indians attacking Rogers, drove them off; the Rangers joined Grant's

company, and all retreated for the fort.   The
shattered remnant of Dalyell's confident forces
arrived at Fort Detroit at eight in the morning, after six hours of marching and desperate
battle, exhausted and crestfallen.   Dalyell
had been slain — an irreparable loss.   The
casualty list was twenty killed and forty-
two wounded.   The Indians had suffered but
slightly.   However, they gained but little
permanent advantage from the victory, as the
fort had still about three hundred effective
men, with ample provisions and ammunition,
and could defy assault and withstand a protracted siege.

In this fight Chippewas and Ottawas took
the leading part.   The Wyandots had, however, at the sound of firing crossed the river,
and the Potawatomis also had joined in the
combat, in spite of the truce so recently made
with Gladwyn.   At the battle of Bloody Run
at least eight hundred warriors were engaged
in the endeavour to cut off Dalyell's men.
There was rejoicing in the Indian villages, and
more British scalps adorned the warriors'
wigwams.   Runners were sent out to the
surrounding nations with news of the victory,
and many recruits were added to Pontiac's
forces.

CHAPTER V

WHILE Fort Detroit was withstanding Pontiac's hordes, the smaller forts and blockhouses scattered throughout the hinterland were faring badly. On the southern shore of Lake Erie, almost directly south of the Detroit river, stood Fort Sandusky—a rude blockhouse surrounded by a stockade. Here were about a dozen men, commanded by Ensign Christopher Paully. The blockhouse could easily have been taken by assault ; but such was not the method of the band of Wyandots in the neighbourhood. They preferred treachery, and, under the guise of friendship, determined to destroy the garrison with no risk to themselves.

On the morning of May 16 Paully was informed that seven Indians wished to confer with him. Four of these were members of the Wyandot tribe, and three belonged to Pontiac's band of Ottawas. The Wyandots were known to Paully, and as he had no news of the situation at Detroit, and no suspicion of danger to himself, he readily admitted them to his quarters. The Indians produced a calumet and handed it to Paully in token of friendship. As the pipe passed from lip to lip a warrior appeared at the door of the room and raised his arm. It was the signal for attack. Immediately Paully was seized by the Indians, two of whom had placed themselves on either side of him. At the same moment a war-whoop rang out and firing began; and as Paully was rushed across the parade-ground he saw the bodies of several of his men, who had been treacherously slain. The sentry had been tomahawked as he stood at arms at the gate; and the sergeant of the little company was killed while working in the garden of the garrison outside the stockade.

When night fell Paully and two or three others, all that remained of the garrison, were placed in canoes, and these were headed for Detroit. As the prisoners looked back over the calm waters of Sandusky Bay, they saw the blockhouse burst into flames. Paully and his men were landed at the Ottawa camp, where a horde of howling Indians, including women and children, beat them and com-

pelled them to dance and sing for the enter-
tainment of the rabble. Preparations were
made to torture Paully to death at the stake ;
but an old squaw, who had recently lost her
husband, was attracted by the handsome, dark-
skinned young ensign, and adopted him in
place of her deceased warrior. Paully's hair
was cut close ; he was dipped into the stream
to wash the white blood from his veins ; and
finally he was dressed and painted as became
an Ottawa brave.

News of the destruction of Fort Sandusky
was brought to Gladwyn by a trader named
La Brosse, a resident of Detroit, and a few
days later a letter was received from Paully
himself. For nearly two months Paully had
to act the part of an Ottawa warrior. But
early in July—Pontiac being in a state of great
rage against the British—his squaw placed
him in a farmhouse for safe keeping. In the
confusion arising out of the attack on Fort
Detroit on the 4th of the month, and the
murder of Captain Campbell, he managed to
escape, by the aid, it is said, of an Indian
maiden. He was pursued to within musket-
shot of the walls of Detroit. When he entered
the fort, so much did he resemble an Indian
that at first he was not recognized.

The next fort to fall into the hands of the Indians was St Joseph, on the east shore of Lake Michigan, at the mouth of the St Joseph river. This was the most inaccessible of the posts on the Great Lakes. The garrison here lived lonely lives. Around them were thick forests and swamps, and in front the desolate waters of the sea-like lake. The Indians about St Joseph had long been under the influence of the French. This place had been visited by La Salle; and here in 1688 the Jesuit Allouez had established a mission. In 1763 the post was held by Ensign Francis Schlosser and fourteen men. For months the little garrison had been without news from the east, when, on May 25, a party of Potawatomis from about Detroit arrived on a pretended visit to their relations living in the village at St Joseph, and asked permission to call on Schlosser. But before a meeting could be arranged, a French trader entered the fort and warned the commandant that the Potawatomis intended to destroy the garrison.

Schlosser at once ordered his sergeant to arm his men, and went among the French settlers seeking their aid. Even while he was addressing them a shrill death-cry rang out— the sentry at the gate had fallen a victim to the tomahawk of a savage. In an instant a howling mob of Potawatomis under their chief Washee were within the stockade. Eleven of the garrison were straightway put to death, and the fort was plundered. Schlosser and the three remaining members of his little band were taken to Detroit by some Foxes who were present with the Potawatomis. On June 10 Schlosser had the good fortune to be exchanged for two chiefs who were prisoners in Fort Detroit.

The Indians did not destroy Fort St Joseph, but left it in charge of the French under Louis Chevalier. Chevalier saved the lives of several British traders, and in every way behaved so admirably that at the close of the Indian war he was given a position of importance under the British, which position he held until the outbreak of the Revolutionary War.

We have seen that when Major Robert Rogers visited Detroit in 1760, one of the French forts first occupied was Miami, situated on the Maumee river, at the commencement of the portage to the Wabash, near the spot where Fort Wayne was afterwards built. At the time of the outbreak of the Pontiac War this fort was held by Ensign Robert Holmes and twelve men. Holmes knew that his position was critical. In 1762 he had reported that the Senecas, Shawnees, and Delawares were plotting to exterminate the British in the Indian country, and he was not surprised when, towards the end of May 1763, he was told by a French trader that Detroit was besieged by the Ottawa Confederacy. But though Holmes was on the alert, and kept his men under arms, he was nevertheless to meet death and his fort was to be captured by treachery. In his desolate wilderness home the young ensign seems to have lost his heart to a handsome young squaw living in the vicinity of the fort. On May 27 she visited him and begged him to accompany her on a mission of mercy—to help to save the life of a sick Indian woman. Having acted as physician to the Indians on former occasions, Holmes thought the request a natural one. The young squaw led him to the Indian village, pointed out the wigwam where the woman was supposed to be, and then left him. As he was about to enter the wigwam two musket-shots rang out, and he fell dead. Three soldiers, who were outside the fort, rushed for the gate, but they were tomahawked before they could reach it. The gate was immediately closed, and the nine

soldiers within the fort made ready for resistance.   With the Indians were two Frenchmen, Jacques Godfroy, whom we have met
before as the ambassador to Pontiac in the
opening days of the siege of Detroit, and one
Miny Chesne;[1] and they had an English
prisoner, a trader named John Welsh, who
had been captured and plundered at the
mouth of the Maumee while on his way to
Detroit.   The Frenchmen called on the garrison to surrender, pointing out how useless it
would be to resist and how dreadful would
be their fate if they were to slay any Indians.
Without a leader, and surrounded as they
were by a large band of savages, the men of
the garrison saw that resistance would be of
no avail.   The gates were thrown open ; the
soldiers marched forth, and were immediately
seized and bound ; and the fort was looted.
With Welsh the captives were taken to the
Ottawa village at Detroit, where they arrived
on June 4, and where Welsh and several of the
soldiers were tortured to death.

A few miles south of the present city of
Lafayette, on the south-east side of the

[1] This is the only recorded instance, except at Detroit, in
which any French took part with the Indians in the capture of
a fort.   And both Godfroy and Miny Chesne had married Indian
women.

Wabash, at the mouth of Wea Creek, stood the little wooden fort of Ouiatanon. It was connected with Fort Miami by a footpath through the forest. It was the most westerly of the British forts in the Ohio country, and might be said to be on the borderland of the territory along the Mississippi, which was still under the government of Louisiana. There was a considerable French settlement, and near by was the principal village of the Weas, a sub-tribe of the Miami nation. The fort was guarded by the usual dozen of men, under the command of Lieutenant Edward Jenkins. In March Jenkins had been warned that an Indian rising was imminent and that soon all the British in the hinterland would be prisoners. The French and Indians in this region were under the influence of the Mississippi officers and traders, who were, in Jenkins's words, ' eternally telling lies to the Indians,' leading them to believe that a great army would soon arrive to recover the forts. Towards the end of May ambassadors arrived at Ouiatanon, either from the Delawares or from Pontiac, bringing war-belts and instructions to the Weas to seize the fort. This, as usual, was achieved by treachery. Jenkins was invited to one of their cabins for a conference.

Totally unaware of the Pontiac conspiracy, or of the fall of St Joseph, Sandusky, or Miami, he accepted the invitation. While passing out of the fort he was seized and bound, and, when taken to the cabin, he saw there several of his soldiers, prisoners like himself. The remaining members of the garrison surrendered, knowing how useless it would be to resist, and under the threat that if one Indian were killed all the British would be put to death. It had been the original intention of the Indians to seize the fort and slaughter the garrison, but, less blood-thirsty than Pontiac's immediate followers, they were won to mercy by two traders, Maisonville and Lorain, who gave them presents on the condition that the garrison should be made prisoners instead of being slain. Jenkins and his men were to have been sent to the Mississippi, but their removal was delayed, and they were quartered on the French inhabitants, and kindly treated by both French and Indians until restored to freedom.

The capture of Forts Miami and Ouiatanon gave the Indians complete control of the route between the western end of Lake Erie and the rivers Ohio and Mississippi. The French traders, who had undoubtedly been instrumental in goading the Indians to hostilities, had now the trade of the Wabash and lower Ohio, and of the tributaries of both, in their own hands. No British trader could venture into the region with impunity; the few who attempted it were plundered and murdered.

The scene of hostilities now shifts to the north. Next to Detroit the most important fort on the Great Lakes west of Niagara was Michilimackinac, situated on the southern shore of the strait connecting Lakes Huron and Michigan. The officer there had supervision of the lesser forts at Sault Ste Marie, Green Bay, and St Joseph. At this time Sault Ste Marie was not occupied by troops. In the preceding winter Lieutenant Jamette had arrived to take command; but fire had broken out in his quarters and destroyed the post, and he and his men had gone back to Michilimackinac, where they still were when the Pontiac War broke out. There were two important Indian tribes in the vicinity of Michilimackinac, the Chippewas and the Ottawas. The Chippewas had populous villages on the island of Mackinaw and at Thunder Bay on Lake Huron. They had as their hunting-grounds the eastern half of the peninsula which is now the state of Michigan. The

Ottawas claimed as their territory the western half of the peninsula, and their chief village was L'Arbre Croche, where the venerable Jesuit priest, Father du Jaunay, had long conducted his mission.

The Indians about Michilimackinac had never taken kindly to the new occupants of the forts in their territory. When the trader Alexander Henry arrived there in 1761, he had found them decidedly hostile. On his journey up the Ottawa he had been warned of the reception in store for him. At Michilimackinac he was waited on by a party of Chippewas headed by their chief, Minavavna, a remarkably sagacious Indian, known to the French as *Le Grand Sauteur*, whose village was situated at Thunder Bay. This chief addressed Henry in most eloquent words, declaring that the Chippewas were the children of the French king, who was asleep, but who would shortly awaken and destroy his enemies. The king of England, he said, had entered into no treaty with the Chippewas and had sent them no presents : they were therefore still at war with him, and until he made such concessions they must look upon the French king as their chief. ' But,' he continued, ' you come unarmed : sleep peacefully!' The pipe of peace was then passed to Henry. After smoking it he bestowed on the Indians some gifts, and they filed out of his presence. Almost immediately on the departure of the Chippewas came some two hundred Ottawas demanding of Henry, and of several other British traders who were also there, ammunition, clothing, and other necessaries for their winter hunt, on credit until spring. The traders refused, and, when threatened by the Indians, they and their employees, some thirty in all, barricaded themselves in a house, and prepared to resist the demands by force of arms. Fortunately, at this critical moment word arrived of a strong British contingent that was approaching from Detroit to take over the fort, and the Ottawas hurriedly left for their villages.

For nearly two years the garrison at Michilimackinac lived in peace. In the spring of 1763 they were resting in a false security. Captain George Etherington, who was in command, heard that the Indians were on the war-path and that the fort was threatened; but he treated the report lightly. It is noteworthy, too, that Henry, who was in daily contact with the French settlers and Indians, and had his agents scattered throughout the

Indian country, saw no cause for alarm. But it happened that towards the end of May news reached the Indians at Michilimackinac of the situation at Detroit, and with the news came a war-belt signifying that they were to destroy the British garrison. A crowd of Indians, chiefly Chippewas and Sacs, presently assembled at the post. This was a usual thing in spring, and would cause no suspicion. The savages, however, had planned to attack the fort on June 4, the birthday of George III. The British were to celebrate the day by sports and feasting, and the Chippewas and Sacs asked to be allowed to entertain the officers with a game of lacrosse. Etherington expressed pleasure at the suggestion, and told the chiefs who waited on him that he would back his friends the Chippewas against their Sac opponents. On the morning of the 4th posts were set up on the wide plain behind the fort, and tribe was soon opposed to tribe. The warriors appeared on the field with moccasined feet, and otherwise naked save for breech-cloths. Hither and thither the ball was batted, thrown, and carried. Player pursued player, tripping, slashing, shouldering each other, and shouting in their excitement as command of the ball passed with the fortunes of the game from Chippewa to Sac and from Sac to Chippewa. Etherington and Lieutenant Leslie were standing near the gate, interested spectators of the game ; and all about, and scattered throughout the fort, were squaws with stoical faces, each holding tight about her a gaudily coloured blanket. The game was at its height, when a player threw the ball to a spot near the gate of the fort. There was a wild rush for it ; and, as the gate was reached, lacrosse sticks were cast aside, the squaws threw open their blankets, and the players seized the tomahawks and knives held out in readiness to them. The shouts of play were changed to war-whoops. Instantly Etherington and Leslie were seized and hurried to a near-by wood. Into the fort the horde dashed. Here stood more squaws with weapons ; and before the garrison had time to seize their arms, Lieutenant Jamette and fifteen soldiers were slain and scalped, and the rest made prisoners, while the French inhabitants stood by, viewing the tragedy with apparent indifference.

Etherington, Leslie, and the soldiers were held close prisoners. A day or two after the capture of the fort a Chippewa chief, *Le Grand Sable*, who had not been present at the

massacre, returned from his wintering-ground.
He entered a hut where a number of British
soldiers were bound hand and foot, and brutally
murdered five of them.   The Ottawas, it will
be noted, had taken no part in the capture
of Michilimackinac.   In fact, owing to the
good offices of their priest, they acted towards
the British as friends in need.   A party of
them from L'Arbre Croche presently arrived
on the scene and prevented further massacre.
Etherington and Leslie were taken from the
hands of the Chippewas and removed to
L'Arbre Croche.   From this place Etherington
sent a message to Green Bay, ordering the
commandant to abandon the fort there.   He
then wrote to Gladwyn at Detroit, giving an
account of what had happened and asking
aid.   This message was carried to Detroit by
Father du Jaunay, who made the journey in
company with seven Ottawas and eight Chippewas commanded by Kinonchanek, a son
of Minavavna.   But, as we know, Gladwyn
was himself in need of assistance, and could
give none.   The prisoners at L'Arbre Croche,
however, were well treated, and finally taken
to Montreal by way of the Ottawa river, under
an escort of friendly Indians.

On the southern shore of Lake Erie, where

the city of Erie now stands, was the fortified post of Presqu'isle, a stockaded fort with several substantial houses. It was considered a strong position, and its commandant, Ensign John Christie, had confidence that he could hold out against any number of Indians that might beset him. The news brought by Cuyler when he visited Presqu'isle, after the disaster at Point Pelée, put Christie on his guard. Presqu'isle had a blockhouse of unusual strength, but it was of wood, and inflammable. To guard against fire, there was left at the top of the building an opening through which water could be poured in any direction. The blockhouse stood on a tongue of land—on the one side a creek, on the other the lake. The most serious weakness of the position was that the banks of the creek and the lake rose in ridges to a considerable height, commanding the blockhouse and affording a convenient shelter for an attacking party within musket range.

Christie had twenty-four men, and believed that he had nothing to fear, when, on June 15, some two hundred Wyandots arrived in the vicinity. These Indians were soon on the ridges, assailing the blockhouse. Arrows tipped with burning tow and balls of blazing pitch rained upon the roof, and the utmost exertions of the garrison were needed to extinguish the fires. Soon the supply of water began to fail. There was a well near by on the parade-ground, but this open space was subject to such a hot fire that no man would venture to cross it. A well was dug in the blockhouse, and the resistance continued. All day the attack was kept up, and during the night there was intermittent firing from the ridges. Another day passed, and at night came a lull in the siege. A demand was made to surrender. An English soldier who had been adopted by the savages, and was aiding them in the attack, cried out that the destruction of the fort was inevitable, that in the morning it would be fired at the top and bottom, and that unless the garrison yielded they would all be burnt to death. Christie asked till morning to consider; and, when morning came, he agreed to yield up the fort on condition that the garrison should be allowed to march to the next post. But as his men filed out they were seized and bound, then cast into canoes and taken to Detroit. Their lives, however, were spared; and early in July, when the Wyandots made with Gladwyn the peace which they afterwards broke, Christie and a number of his men were the first prisoners given up.

A few miles inland, south of Presqu'isle, on the trade-route leading to Fort Pitt, was a rude blockhouse known as Le Bœuf. This post was at the end of the portage from Lake Erie, on Alleghany Creek, where the canoe navigation of the Ohio valley began. Here were stationed Ensign George Price and thirteen men. On June 18 a band of Indians arrived before Le Bœuf and attacked it with muskets and fire-arrows. The building was soon in flames. As the walls smoked and crackled the savages danced in wild glee before the gate, intending to shoot down the defenders as they came out. But there was a window at the rear of the blockhouse, through which the garrison escaped to the neighbouring forest. When night fell the party became separated. Some of them reached Fort Venango two days later, only to find it in ruins. Price and seven men laboriously toiled through the forest to Fort Pitt, where they arrived on June 26. Ultimately, all save two of the garrison of Fort Le Bœuf reached safety.

The circumstances attending the destruction of Fort Venango on June 20 are but

vaguely known.   This fort, situated near the
site of the present city of Franklin, had long
been a centre of Indian trade.   In the days of
the French occupation it was known as Fort
Machault.   After the French abandoned the
place in the summer of 1760 a new fort had
been erected and named Venango.   In 1763
there was a small garrison here under Lieutenant Gordon.   For a time all that was
known of its fate was reported by the fugitives
from Le Bœuf and a soldier named Gray, who
had escaped from Presqu'isle.   These fugitives
had found Venango completely destroyed, and,
in the ruins, the blackened bones of the
garrison.   It was afterwards learned that the
attacking Indians were Senecas, and that
they had tortured the commandant to death
over a slow fire, after compelling him to
write down the reason for the attack.   It was
threefold : (1) the British charged exorbitant prices for powder, shot, and clothing ;
(2) when Indians were ill-treated by British
soldiers they could obtain no redress ; (3) con-
trary to the wishes of the Indians, forts were
being built in their country, and these could
mean but one thing—the determination of the
invaders to deprive them of their hunting-
grounds.

With the fall of Presqu'isle, Le Bœuf, and Venango, the trade-route between Lake Erie and Fort Pitt was closed. Save for Detroit, Niagara, and Pitt, not a British fort remained in the great hinterland; and the soldiers at these three strong positions could leave the shelter of the palisades only at the risk of their lives. Meanwhile, the frontiers of the British settlements, as well as the forts, were being raided. Homes were burnt and the inmates massacred. Traders were plundered and slain. From the eastern slopes of the Alleghanies to the Mississippi no British life was safe.

CHAPTER VI

THE RELIEF OF FORT PITT

ON the tongue of land at the confluence of the Monongahela and Alleghany rivers stood Fort Pitt, on the site of the old French fort Duquesne. It was remote from any centre of population, but was favourably situated for defence, and so strongly garrisoned that those in charge of it had little to fear from any attempts of the Indians to capture it. Floods had recently destroyed part of the ramparts, but these had been repaired and a parapet of logs raised above them.

Captain Simeon Ecuyer, a Swiss soldier in the service of Great Britain and an officer of keen intelligence and tried courage, was in charge of Fort Pitt. He knew the Indians. He had quickly realized that danger threatened his wilderness post, and had left nothing undone to make it secure. On the fourth day of May, Ecuyer had written to Colonel Henry Bouquet, who was stationed

at Philadelphia, saying that he had received
word from Gladwyn that he 'was surrounded
by rascals.' Ecuyer did not treat this alarm
lightly. He not only repaired the ramparts
and made them stronger, but also erected
palisades within them to surround the dwell-
ings. Everything near the fort that could
give shelter to a lurking foe was levelled to
the ground. There were in Fort Pitt at this
time about a hundred women and their
children—families of settlers who had come
to the fertile Ohio valley to take up homes.
These were provided with shelter in houses
made shot-proof. Small-pox had broken out
in the garrison, and a hospital was prepared
under the drawbridge, where the patients in
time of siege would be in no danger from
musket-balls or arrows. But the best defence
of Fort Pitt was the capacity of Ecuyer—
brave, humorous, foresighted ; a host in himself—giving courage to his men and making
even the women and children think lightly of
the power of the Indians.

It was nearly three weeks after the siege of
Detroit had begun that the savages appeared
in force about Fort Pitt. On May 27 a large
band of Indians came down the Alleghany
bearing packs of furs, in payment for which

they demanded guns, knives, tomahawks, powder, and shot, and would take nothing else. Soon after their departure word was brought to Ecuyer of the murder of some traders and settlers not far from the fort. From that time until the beginning of August it was hazardous for any one to venture outside the walls; but for nearly a month no attack was to be made on the fort itself. However, as news of the capture of the other forts reached the garrison, and as nearly all the messengers sent to the east were either slain or forced to return, it was evident that, in delaying the attack on Fort Pitt, the Indians were merely gathering strength for a supreme effort against the strongest position in the Indian territory.

On June 22 a large body of Indians assembled in the forest about the fort, and, creeping stealthily within range of its walls, opened fire from every side. It was the garrison's first experience of attack; some of the soldiers proved a trifle overbold, and two of them were killed. The firing, however, lasted but a short time. Ecuyer selected a spot where the smoke of the muskets was thickest, and threw shells from his howitzers into the midst of the warriors, scattering them in hurried flight.   On the following day a party came within speaking distance, and their leader, Turtle's Heart, a Delaware chief, informed Ecuyer that all the western and northern forts had been cut off, and that a host of warriors were coming to destroy Fort Pitt and its garrison.   He begged Ecuyer to withdraw the inmates of the fort while there was yet time.   He would see to it that they were protected on their way to the eastern settlements.   He added that when the Ottawas and their allies arrived, all hope for the lives of the inhabitants of Fort Pitt would be at an end.   All this Turtle's Heart told Ecuyer out of ' love for the British.' The British officer, with fine humour, thanked him for his consideration for the garrison, but told him that he could hold out against all the Indians in the woods.   He could be as gener-ous as Turtle's Heart, and so warned him that the British were coming to relieve Fort Pitt with six thousand men ;   that an army of three thousand was ascending the Great Lakes to punish the Ottawa Confederacy ;   and that still another force of three thousand had gone to the frontiers of Virginia.   ' Therefore,' he said, ' take pity on your women and children, and get out of the way as soon as possible.

We have told you this in confidence, out of our
great solicitude, lest any of you should be
hurt ; and,' he added, ' we hope that you will
not tell the other Indians, lest they should
escape from our vengeance.' The howitzers
and the story of the approaching hosts had
their effect, and the Indians vanished into
the surrounding forest. For another month
Fort Pitt had comparative peace, and the
garrison patiently but watchfully awaited a
relieving force which Amherst was sending.
In the meantime news came of the destruction
of Presqu'isle, Le Bœuf, and Venango ; and
the fate of the garrisons, particularly at the
last post, warned the inhabitants of Fort Pitt
what they might expect if they should fall
into the hands of the Indians.

On July 26 some Indian ambassadors,
among them Turtle's Heart, came to the post
with a flag of truce. They were loud in their
protestations of friendship, and once more
solicitous for the safety of the garrison. The
Ottawas, they said, were coming in a vast
horde, to ' seize and eat up everything ' that
came in their way. The garrison's only hope
of escape would be to vacate the fort speedily
and ' go home to their wives and children.'
Ecuyer replied that he would never abandon

his position ' as long as a white man lives in
America.' He despised the Ottawas, he said,
and was ' very much surprised at our brothers
the Delawares for proposing to us to leave this
place and go home. This is our home.' His
humour was once more in evidence in the
warning he gave the Indians against repeating
their attack on the fort : ' I will throw bomb-
shells, which will burst and blow you to atoms,
and fire cannon among you, loaded with a
whole bagful of bullets. Therefore take care,
for I don't want to hurt you.'

The Indians now gave up all hope of capturing Fort Pitt by deception, and prepared to
take it by assault. That very night they stole
within range, dug shelter-pits in the banks of
the Alleghany and Monongahela, and at daybreak began a vigorous attack on the garrison.
Musket-balls came whistling over the ramparts and smote every point where a soldier
showed himself. The shrieking balls and
the wild war-whoops of the assailants greatly
alarmed the women and children ; but never
for a moment was the fort in real danger
or did Ecuyer or his men fear disaster.
So carefully had the commandant seen to
his defences, that, although hundreds of
missiles fell within the confines of the fort,

only one man was killed and only seven were wounded. Ecuyer himself was among the wounded : one of two arrows that fell within the fort had, to use his own words, ' the insolence to make free ' with his ' left leg.' From July 27 to August 1 this horde of Delawares, Shawnees, Wyandots, and Mingoes kept up the attack. Then, without apparent cause, as suddenly as they had arrived, they all disappeared. To the garrison the relief from constant vigil, anxious days, and sleepless nights was most welcome.

The reason for this sudden relief was that the red men had learned of a rich prize for them, now approaching Fort Pitt. Bouquet, with a party of soldiers, was among the defiles of the Alleghanies. The fort could wait ; the Indians would endeavour to annihilate Bouquet's force as they had annihilated Braddock's army in the same region eight years before ; and if successful, they could then at their leisure return to Fort Pitt and starve it out or take it by assault.

In June, when Amherst had finally come to the conclusion that he had a real war on his hands—and had, as we have seen, dispatched Dalyell to Detroit—he had, at the same time, sent orders to Colonel Bouquet to get ready a force for the relief of Fort Pitt. Bouquet, like Ecuyer, was a Swiss soldier, and the best man in America for this particular task. After seven years' experience in border warfare he was as skilled in woodcraft as the Indians themselves. He had now to lead a force over the road, two hundred odd miles long, which connected Fort Pitt with Carlisle, his point of departure in Pennsylvania; but every foot of the road was known to him. In 1758, when serving under General Forbes, he had directed the construction of this road, and knew the strength of every fort and blockhouse on the way; even the rivers and creeks and morasses and defiles were familiar to him. Best of all, he had a courage and a military knowledge that inspired confidence in his men and officers. Cool, calculating, foreseeing, dauntlessly brave—there was not in the New World at this time a better soldier than this heroic Swiss.

Amherst was in a bad way for troops. The only available forces for the relief of Fort Pitt were 242 men of the 42nd Highlanders—the famous Black Watch—with 133 of the 77th (Montgomery's) Highlanders, and some Royal Americans. These, with a few volunteers, made up a contingent 550 strong. It was a

force all too small for the task before it, and
the majority of the soldiers had but recently
arrived from the West Indies and were in
wretched health.

Bouquet had sent instructions to Carlisle
to have supplies ready for him and sufficient
wagons assembled there for the expedition,
but when he reached the place at the end of
June he found that nothing had been done.
The frontier was in a state of paralysis from
panic. Over the entire stretch of country
from Fort Pitt the Indians were on the war-
path. Every day brought tragic stories of
the murder of settlers and the destruction of
their homes. There was no safety outside
the precincts of the feeble forts that dotted
the Indian territory. Bouquet had hoped for
help from the settlers and government of
Pennsylvania; but the settlers thought only
of immediate safety, and the government was
criminally negligent in leaving the frontier
of the state unprotected, and would vote
neither men nor money for defence. But they
must be saved in spite of themselves. By
energetic efforts, in eighteen days after his
arrival at Carlisle, Bouquet was ready for the
march. He began his campaign with a wise
precaution. The last important fort on the

COLONEL HENRY BOUQUET

From a contemporary painting

road to Pitt was Ligonier, about one hundred and fifty miles from Carlisle. It would be necessary to use this post as a base; but it was beset by Indians and in danger of being captured. Lieutenant Archibald Blane in charge of it was making a gallant defence against a horde of savages. Bouquet, while waiting at Carlisle, engaged guides and sent in advance thirty Highlanders, carefully selected men, to strengthen the garrison under Blane. These, by keeping off the main trail and using every precaution, succeeded in reaching the fort without mishap.

Bouquet led his force westward. Sixty of his soldiers were so ill that they were unable to march and had to be carried in wagons. It was intended that the sick should take the place of the men now in Forts Bedford and Ligonier, and thus help to guard the rear. The road was found to be in frightful condition. The spring freshets had cut it up; deep gullies crossed the path; and the bridges over the streams had been in most cases washed away. As the little army advanced, panic-stricken settlers by the way told stories of the destruction of homes and the slaughter of friends. Fort Bedford, where Captain Lewis Ourry was in command, was reached

on the 25th.   Here three days were spent, and
thirty more guides were secured to serve as an
advance-guard of scouts and give warning of
the presence of enemies.   Bouquet had tried
his Highlanders at this work ; but they were
unfamiliar with the forest, and, as they in-
variably got lost, were of no value as scouts.
Leaving his invalided officers and men at
Bedford, Bouquet, with horses rested and men
refreshed, pressed forward and arrived at
Ligonier on August 2.   Preparations had now
to be made for the final dash to Fort Pitt, fifty
odd miles away, over a path that was beset by
savages, who also occupied all the important
passes.   It would be impossible to get through
without a battle—a wilderness battle—and
the thought of the Braddock disaster was in
the minds of all.   But Bouquet was not a
Braddock, and he was experienced in Indian
warfare.   To attempt to pass ambuscades
with a long train of cumbersome wagons
would be to invite disaster ; so he discarded
his wagons and heavier stores, and having
made ready three hundred and forty pack-
horses loaded with flour, he decided to set
out from Ligonier on the 4th of August.   It
was planned to reach Bushy Creek—'Bushy
Run,' as Bouquet called it—on the following

day, and there rest and refresh horses and men. In the night a dash would be made through the dangerous defile at Turtle Creek; and, if the high broken country at this point could be passed without mishap, the rest of the way could be easily won.

At daylight the troops were up and off. It was an oppressively hot August morning, and no breath of wind stirred the forest. Over the rough road trudged the long line of sweltering men. In advance were the scouts; then followed several light companies of the Black Watch; then the main body of the little army; and in the rear came the toiling pack-horses. Until noon the soldiers marched, panting and tortured by mosquitoes, but buoyed up by the hope that at Bushy Run they would be able to quench their burning thirst and rest until nightfall. By one o'clock in the afternoon they had covered seventeen miles and were within a mile and a half of their objective point. Suddenly in their front they heard the sharp reports of muskets; the firing grew in intensity: the advance-guard was evidently in contact with a considerable body of Indians. Two light companies were rushed forward to their support, and with fixed bayonets cleared the path. This, however, was but a temporary success. The Indians merely changed their position and appeared on the flanks in increased numbers. From the shelter of trees the foe were creating havoc among the exposed troops, and a general charge was necessary. Highlanders and Royal Americans, acting under the directing eye of Bouquet, again drove the Indians back with the bayonet. Scarcely had this been accomplished when a fusillade was heard in the rear. The convoy was attacked, and it was necessary to fall back to its support. Until nightfall, around a bit of elevated ground—called Edge Hill by Bouquet—on which the convoy was drawn up, the battle was waged. About the pack-horses and stores the soldiers valiantly fought for seven hours against their invisible foe. At length darkness fell, and the exhausted troops could take stock of their losses and snatch a brief, broken rest. In this day of battle two officers were killed and four wounded, and sixty of the rank and file were killed or wounded.

Flour-bags were piled in a circle, and within this the wounded were placed. Throughout the night a careful watch was kept ; but the enemy made no attack during the darkness, merely firing an occasional shot and from time

to time uttering defiant yells. They were
confident that Bouquet's force would be an
easy prey, and waited for daylight to renew
the battle.

The soldiers had played a heroic part.
Though unused to forest warfare, they had
been cool as veterans in Indian fighting, and
not a man had fired a shot without orders.
But the bravest of them looked to the morning
with dread. They had barely been able to
hold their own on this day, and by morning
the Indians would undoubtedly be greatly
strengthened. The cries and moans of the
wounded vividly reminded them of what had
already happened. Besides, they were worn
out with marching and fighting ; worse than
physical fatigue and more trying than the
enemy's bullets was torturing thirst ; and not
a drop of water could be obtained at the place
where they were hemmed in.

By the flickering light of a candle Bouquet
penned one of the noblest letters ever written
by a soldier in time of battle. He could
hardly hope for success, and defeat meant the
most horrible of deaths ; but he had no craven
spirit, and his report to Amherst was that of
a true soldier—a man ' whose business it is
to die.' After giving a detailed account of the

occurrences leading up to this attack and a
calm statement of the events of the day, and
paying a tribute to his officers, whose conduct,
he said, ' is much above my praise,' he added :
' Whatever our fate may be, I thought it
necessary to give Your Excellency this information. . . . I fear unsurmountable diffi-
culties in protecting and transporting our provisions, being already so much weakened by
the loss in this day of men and horses.'   Sending a messenger back with this dispatch, he
set himself to plan for the morrow.

At daybreak from the surrounding wood
the terrifying war-cries of the Indians fell
on the ears of the troops.   Slowly the shrill
yells came nearer ;   the Indians were endeavouring to strike terror into the hearts
of their foes before renewing the fight, knowing that troops in dread of death are already
half beaten.   When within five hundred yards
of the centre of the camp the Indians began
firing.   The troops replied with great steadi-
ness.   This continued until ten in the morning.
The wounded within the barricade lay listening
to the sounds of battle, ever increasing in
volume, and the fate of Braddock's men rose
before them.   It seemed certain that their suf-
ferings must end in death—and what a death !

The pack-horses, tethered at a little distance from the barricade, offered an easy target, against which the Indians soon directed their fire, and the piteous cries of the wounded animals added to the tumult of the battle. Some of the horses, maddened by wounds, broke their fastenings and galloped into the forest. But the kilted Highlanders and the red-coated Royal Americans gallantly fought on. Their ranks were being thinned ; the fatiguing work of the previous day was telling on them ; their throats were parched and their tongues swollen for want of water. Bouquet surveyed the field. He saw his men weakening under the terrible strain, and realized that something must be done promptly. The Indians were each moment becoming bolder, pressing ever nearer and nearer.

Then he conceived one of the most brilliant movements known in Indian warfare. He ordered two companies, which were in the most exposed part of the field, to fall back as though retreating within the circle that defended the hill. At the same time the troops on the right and left opened their files, and, as if to cover the retreat, occupied the space vacated in a thinly extended line. The strategy worked even better than Bouquet had expected. The

yelling Indians, eager for slaughter and believing that the entire command was at their
mercy, rushed pell-mell from their shelter,
firing sharp volleys into the protecting files.
These were forced back, and the savages
dashed forward for the barricade which
sheltered the wounded. Meanwhile the two
companies had taken position on the right,
and from a sheltering hill that concealed them
from the enemy they poured an effective fire
into the savages. The astonished Indians
replied, but with little effect, and before they
could reload the Highlanders were on them
with the bayonet. The red men then saw
that they had fallen into a trap, and turned to
flee. But suddenly on their left two more
companies rose from ambush and sent a storm
of bullets into the retreating savages, while
the Highlanders and Royal Americans dashed
after them with fixed bayonets. The Indians
at other parts of the circle, seeing their comrades in flight, scattered into the forest. The
defiant war-cries ceased and the muskets were
silent. The victory was complete : Bouquet
had beaten the Indians in their own woods and
at their own game. About sixty of the enemy
lay dead and as many more wounded. In the
two days of battle the British had fifty killed,

sixty wounded, and five missing. It was a heavy price ; but this victory broke the back of the Indian war.

Many horses had been killed or had strayed away, and it was impossible to transport all the stores to Fort Pitt. What could not be carried with the force was destroyed, and the victors moved on to Bushy Creek, at a slow pace on account of the wounded. No sooner had they pitched their tents at the creek than some of the enemy again appeared; the Highlanders, however, without waiting for the word of command, scattered them with the bayonet. On the following day the march began for Fort Pitt. Three days later, on August 10, the garrison of that fort heard the skirl of the bagpipes and the beat of the drum, and saw through the forest the plaids and plumes of the Highlanders and the red coats of the Royal Americans. The gate was thrown open, and the victors of Edge Hill marched in to the welcome of the men and women who for several months had had no news from their friends in the east.

Bouquet had been instructed to invade the Ohio country and teach the Shawnees and Delawares a lesson. But his men were worn out, half of them were unfit for service, and so deficient was he in horses and supplies that this task had to be abandoned for the present year.

Pennsylvania and Virginia rejoiced. This triumph meant much to them. Their borders would now be safe, but for occasional scalping parties. Amherst was delighted, and took to himself much of the credit of Bouquet's victory. He congratulated the noble Swiss officer on his victory over ' a band of savages that would have been very formidable against any troops but such as you had with you.' But it was not the troops that won the battle; it was Bouquet. In the hands of a Braddock, a Loudoun, an Abercromby, these war-worn veterans would have met a fate such as befell Braddock's troops. But Bouquet animated every man with his own spirit ; he knew how to fight Indians ; and at the critical moment —' the fatal five minutes between victory and defeat '—he proved himself the equal of any soldier who ever battled against the red men in North America.

CHAPTER VII

DETROIT ONCE MORE

WHILE Fort Pitt was holding out against the Ohio Indians and Bouquet was forcing his way through the defiles of the Alleghanies to its relief, Fort Detroit was still in a state of siege. The defeat of Dalyell's force at Bloody Run had given the Indians a greater degree of confidence. They had not dared, however, to make a general assault, but had merely kept the garrison aware of their presence by desultory and irritating attacks.

Nothing of importance took place until September 3. On this day the little *Gladwyn*, which had gone to the Niagara with dispatches, entered the Detroit river on her return trip. She was in charge of Captain Horst, who was assisted by Jacobs as mate, and a crew of ten men. There were likewise on board six Iroquois Indians. It was a calm morning; and as the vessel lay with idly flapping sails waiting for a wind, the Iroquois asked permission to stretch their limbs on shore. Horst foolishly granted their request, and as soon as they had made a landing they disappeared into the forest, and no doubt hurried to Pontiac's warriors to let them know how weakly manned was the schooner. The weather continued calm, and by nightfall the *Gladwyn* was still nine miles below the fort. As darkness fell on that moonless night the captain, alarmed at the flight of the Iroquois, posted a careful guard and had his cannon at bow and stern made ready to resist attack. So dark was the night that it was impossible to discern objects at any distance. Along the black shore Indians were gathering, and soon a fleet of canoes containing over three hundred warriors was slowly and silently moving towards the becalmed *Gladwyn*. So noiseless was their approach that they were within a few yards of the vessel before a watchful sentry, the boatswain, discerned them. At his warning cry the crew leapt to their quarters. The bow gun thundered out, and its flash gave the little band on the boat a momentary glimpse of a horde of painted enemies. There was no time to reload the gun. The canoes were all about the schooner, and yelling warriors were clambering over the stern and

bow and swarming on the deck. The crew
discharged their muskets into the savages,
and then seized spears and hatchets and
rushed madly at them, striking and stabbing—
determined at least to sell their lives dearly.
For a moment the Indians in the black darkness shrank back from the fierce attack. But
already Horst was killed and several of the
crew were down with mortal wounds. The
vessel seemed lost when Jacobs—a dare-devil
seaman—now in command, ordered his men
to blow up the vessel. A Wyandot brave
with some knowledge of English caught the
words and shouted a warning to his comrades.
In an instant every warrior was over the side
of the vessel, paddling or swimming to get to
safety. When morning broke not an Indian
was to be seen, and the little *Gladwyn* sailed
in triumph to Fort Detroit. So greatly was
the gallantry of her crew appreciated that
Amherst had a special medal struck and given
to each of the survivors.

Meanwhile, at Niagara, supplies were being
conveyed over the portage between the lower
landing (now Lewiston) and Fort Schlosser,
in readiness for transport to the western posts.
The Senecas claimed the territory about
Niagara, and the invasion of their land had

greatly irritated them. They particularly
resented the act of certain squatters who,
without their consent, had settled along
the Niagara portage. Fort Niagara was too
strong to be taken by assault; but the
Senecas hoped, by biding their time, to strike
a deadly blow against parties conveying goods
over the portage. The opportunity came on
September 14. On this day a sergeant and
twenty-eight men were engaged in escorting
down to the landing a wagon-train and pack-
horses which had gone up to Fort Schlosser
the day before loaded with supplies. The
journey up the river had been successfully
made, and the party were returning, off their
guard and without the slightest thought of
danger. But their every movement had been
watched by Indian scouts; and, at the Devil's
Hole, a short distance below the falls, five
hundred warriors lay in ambush. Slowly
the returning provision-train wound its way
along the bank of the Niagara. On the right
were high cliffs, thickly wooded; on the left
a precipice, whose base was fretted by the
furious river. In the ears of the soldiers and
drivers sounded the thunderous roar of the
mighty cataract. As men and horses threaded
their way past the Devil's Hole savage yells

`burst from the thick wood on their right, and simultaneously a fusillade from a hundred muskets. The terrified horses sprang over the cliffs, dragging wagons and drivers with them. When the smoke cleared and the savages rushed forward, not a living member of the escort nor a driver was to be seen. The leader of the escort, Philip Stedman, had grasped the critical character of the situation at the first outcry, and, putting spurs to his horse, had dashed into the bushes. A warrior had seized his rein; but Stedman had struck him down and galloped free for Fort Schlosser. A drummer-boy, in terror of his life, had leapt over the cliff. By good fortune his drum-strap caught on the branch of a dense tree; here he remained suspended until the Indians left the spot, when he extricated himself. One of the teamsters also escaped. He was wounded, but managed to roll into the bushes, and found concealment in the thick under-growth. The terrific musketry fire was heard at the lower landing, where a body of troops of the 6oth and 8oth regiments were encamped. The soldiers hastily armed themselves and in great disorder rushed to the aid of the convoy. But the Indians were not now at the Devil's Hole. The murderous work completed there, they had taken up a position in a thick wood half a mile farther down, where they silently waited. They had chosen well their place of concealment; and the soldiers in their excitement walked into the trap set for them. Suddenly the ominous war-cries broke out, and before the troops could turn to face the foe a storm of bullets had swept their left flank. Then the warriors dashed from their ambush, tomahawking the living and scalping both dead and dying. In a few minutes five officers and seventy-six of the rank and file were killed and eight wounded, and out of a force of over one hundred men only twenty escaped unhurt. The news of this second disaster brought Major Wilkins up from Fort Niagara, with every available man, to chastise the Indians. But when Wilkins and his men arrived at the gruesome scene of the massacre not a red man was to be found. The Indians had disappeared into the forest, after having stripped their victims even of clothing. With a heavy heart the troops marched back to Niagara, mourning the loss of many gallant comrades. This was the greatest disaster, in loss of life, of the Pontiac War; but, like the defeat of Dalyell, it had little effect on the progress of the campaign. The Indians did not follow it up ; with scalps and plunder they returned to their villages to exult in wild orgies over the victory.

Detroit was still besieged ; but the Indians were beginning to weaken, and for the most part had given up hope of forcing the garrison to surrender. They had been depending almost wholly on the settlement for sustenance, and provisions were running low. Ammunition, too, was well-nigh exhausted. They had replenished their supply during the summer by the captures they had made, by the plundering of traders, and by purchase or gift from the French of the Mississippi. Now they had little hope of capturing more supply-boats ; the traders were holding aloof ; and, since the arrival of definite news of the surrender to Great Britain by France of the region east of the Mississippi, supplies from the French had been stopped. If the Indians were to escape starvation they must scatter to their hunting-grounds. There was another reason why many of the chiefs deemed it wise to leave the vicinity of Detroit. They had learned that Major Wilkins was on his way from Niagara with a strong force and a fleet of bateaux loaded with ammunition and supplies. So, early in October, the Potawatomis,

Wyandots, and Chippewas held a council
and concluded to bury the hatchet and make
peace with Gladwyn. On the 12th of the
month a delegation from these tribes came
to the fort bearing a pipe of peace. Gladwyn
knew from experience how little they were to
be trusted, but he gave them a seemingly
cordial welcome. A chief named Wapocomo-
guth acted as spokesman, and stated that the
tribes represented regretted 'their bad conduct' and were ready to enter into a treaty
of peace. Gladwyn replied that it was not
in his power to grant peace to Indians who
without cause had attacked the troops of
their father the king of England; only
the commander-in-chief could do that; but
he consented to a cessation of hostilities.
He did this the more willingly as the fort
was short of food, and the truce would
give him a chance to lay in a fresh stock of
provisions.

As the autumn frosts were colouring the
maples with brilliant hues, the Potawatomis,
Wyandots, and Chippewas set out for fields
where game was plentiful; but for a time
Pontiac with his Ottawas remained, threatening the garrison, and still strong in his determination to continue the siege. During the

summer he had sent ambassadors to Fort
Chartres on the Mississippi asking aid in
fighting what he asserted to be the battle
of the French traders. Towards the end of
July the messengers had returned with word
from Neyon de Villiers, the commandant of
Fort Chartres, saying that he must await
more definite news as to whether peace had
been concluded between France and England.
Pontiac still hoped ; and, after his allies had
deserted, he waited at his camp above Detroit
for further word from Neyon.   On the last day
of October Louis Césair Dequindre arrived at
Detroit from Fort Chartres, with the crushing
answer that Neyon de Villiers could give him no
aid.   England and France were at peace, and
Neyon advised the Ottawas—no doubt with
reluctance, and only because of the demand
of Amherst—to bury the hatchet and give up
the useless contest.   To continue the struggle
for the present would be vain.   Pontiac,
though enraged by the desertion of his allies,
and by what seemed to him the cowardly
conduct of the French, determined at once
to accept the situation, sue for peace, and
lay plans for future action.   So far he had
been fighting ostensibly for the restoration of
French rule.   In future, whatever scheme he

might devise, his struggle must be solely in the interests of the red man. Next day he sent a letter to Gladwyn begging that the past might be forgotten. His young men, he said, had buried their hatchets, and he declared himself ready not only to make peace, but also to ' send to all the nations concerned in the war ' telling them to cease hostilities. No trust could Gladwyn put in Pontiac's words ; yet he assumed a friendly bearing towards the treacherous conspirator, who for nearly six months had given him no rest. Gladwyn's views of the situation at this time are well shown in a report he made to Amherst. The Indians, he said, had lost many of their best warriors, and would not be likely again to show a united front. It was in this report that he made the suggestion, unique in warfare, of destroying the Indians by the free sale of rum to them. ' If y' Excellency,' he wrote, ' still intends to punish them further for their barbarities, it may easily be done without any expense to the Crown, by permitting a free sale of rum, which will destroy them more effectually than fire and sword.' He thought that the French had been the real plotters of the Indian war : ' I don't imagine there will be any danger of their [the Indians]

breaking out again, provided some examples
are made of our good friends, the French, who
set them on.'

Pontiac and his band of savages paddled
southward for the Maumee, and spent the
winter among the Indians along its upper
waters.   Again he broke his plighted word
and plotted a new confederacy, greater than
the Three Fires, and sent messengers with
wampum belts and red hatchets to all the
tribes as far south as the mouth of the Mississippi and as far north as the Red River.   But
his glory had departed.   He could call; but
the warriors would not come when he summoned them.

Fort Detroit was freed from hostile Indians,
and the soldiers could go to rest without ex-
pecting to hear the call to arms.   But before
the year closed it was to be the witness of still
another tragedy.   Two or three weeks after
the massacre at the Devil's Hole, Major
Wilkins with some six hundred troops started
from Fort Schlosser with a fleet of bateaux
for Detroit.   No care seems to have been
taken to send out scouts to learn if the
forest bordering the river above the falls was
free from Indians, and, as the bateaux were
slowly making their way against the swift

stream towards Lake Erie, they were savagely attacked from the western bank by Indians in such force that Wilkins was compelled to retreat to Fort Schlosser. It was not until November that another attempt was made to send troops and provisions to Detroit. Early in this month Wilkins once more set out from Fort Schlosser, this time with forty-six bateaux heavily laden with troops, provisions, and ammunition. While they were in Lake Erie there arose one of the sudden storms so prevalent on the Great Lakes in autumn. Instead of creeping along the shore, the bateaux were in mid-lake, and before a landing could be made the gale was on them in all its fury. There was a wild race for land; but the choppy, turbulent sea beat upon the boats, of which some were swamped and the crews plunged into the chilly waters. They were opposite a forbidding shore, called by Wilkins Long Beach, but there was no time to look for a harbour. An attempt was made to land, with disastrous results. In all sixteen boats were sunk; three officers, four sergeants, and sixty-three privates were drowned. The thirty bateaux brought ashore were in a sinking condition; half the provisions were lost and the remainder water-soaked. The

journey to Detroit was out of the question.
The few provisions saved would not last
the remnant of Wilkins's own soldiers for a
month, and the ammunition was almost
entirely lost.   Even if they succeeded in
arriving safely at Detroit, they would only
be an added burden to Gladwyn; and so,
sick at heart from failure and the loss of
comrades, the survivors beat their way back
to the Niagara.

A week or two later a messenger arrived at
Fort Detroit bearing news of the disaster.
The scarcity of provisions at Detroit was such
that Gladwyn decided to reduce his garrison.
Keeping about two hundred men in the fort,
he sent the rest to Niagara.   Then the force
remaining at Detroit braced themselves to
endure a hard, lonely winter.   Theirs was not
a pleasant lot.   Never was garrison duty en-
joyable during winter in the northern parts
of North America, but in previous winters
at Detroit the friendly intercourse between
the soldiers and the settlers had made the
season not unbearable.   Now, so many of
the French had been sympathizers with the
besieging Indians, and, indeed, active in
aiding them, that the old relations could
not be resumed.   So, during this winter of

1763-64, the garrison for the most part held
aloof from the French settlers, and performed their weary round of military duties,
longing for spring and the sight of a relieving
force.

CHAPTER VIII

WINDING UP THE INDIAN WAR

AMHERST was weary of America. Early in
the summer of 1763 he had asked to be relieved of his command; but it was not until
October that General Thomas Gage, then in
charge of the government of Montreal, was
appointed to succeed him, and not until
November 17, the day after Gage arrived in
New York, that Amherst sailed for England.

The new commander-in-chief was not as
great a general as Amherst. It is doubtful
if he could have planned and brought to a
successful conclusion such campaigns as the
siege of Louisbourg and the threefold march
of 1760 on Montreal, which have given his
predecessor a high place in the military history of North America. But Gage was better
suited for winding up the Indian war. He
knew the value of the officers familiar with the
Indian tribes, and was ready to act on their
advice. Amherst had not done this, and his

best officers were now anxious to resign.
George Croghan had resigned as assistant
superintendent of Indian Affairs, but was later
induced by Gage to remain in office. Gladwyn
was ' heartily wearied ' of his command and
hoped to ' be relieved soon ' ; Blane and Ourry
were tired of their posts ; and the brave
Ecuyer was writing in despair : ' For God's
sake, let me go and raise cabbages.' Bouquet,
too, although determined to see the war to a
conclusion, was not satisfied with the situation.

Meanwhile, Sir William Johnson was not
idle among the tribes of the Six Nations.   The
failure of Pontiac to reduce Fort Detroit and
the victory of Bouquet at Edge Hill had convinced the Iroquois that ultimately the British
would triumph, and, eager to be on the winning side, they consented to take the field
against the Shawnees and Delawares.   In the
middle of February 1764, through Johnson's
influence and by his aid, two hundred
Tuscaroras and Oneidas, under a half-breed,
Captain Montour, marched westward.   Near
the main branch of the Susquehanna they
surprised forty Delawares, on a scalping
expedition against the British settlements,
and made prisoners of the entire party.   A
few weeks later a number of Mohawks led by

Joseph Brant (Thayendanegea) put another band of Delawares to rout, killing their chief and taking three prisoners. These attacks of the Iroquois disheartened the Shawnees and Delawares and greatly alarmed the Senecas, who, trembling lest their own country should be laid waste, sent a deputation of four hundred of their chief men to Johnson Hall —Sir William Johnson's residence on the Mohawk—to sue for peace. It was agreed that the Senecas should at once stop all hostilities, never again take up arms against the British, deliver up all prisoners at Johnson Hall, cede to His Majesty the Niagara carrying-place, allow the free passage of troops through their country, renounce all intercourse with the Delawares and Shawnees, and assist the British in punishing them. Thus, early in 1764, through the energy and diplomacy of Sir William Johnson, the powerful Senecas were brought to terms.

With the opening of spring preparations began in earnest for a twofold invasion of the Indian country. One army was to proceed to Detroit by way of Niagara and the Lakes, and another from Fort Pitt was to take the field against the Delawares and the Shawnees. To Colonel John Bradstreet, who in 1758 had

won distinction by his capture of Fort
Frontenac, was assigned the command of
the contingent that was to go to Detroit.
Bradstreet was to punish the Wyandots of
Sandusky, and likewise the members of the
Ottawa Confederacy if he should find them
hostile. He was also to relieve Gladwyn and
re-garrison the forts captured by the Indians
in 1763. Bradstreet left Albany in June
with a large force of colonial troops and
regulars, including three hundred French
Canadians from the St Lawrence, whom Gage
had thought it wise to have enlisted, in order
to impress upon the Indians that they need
no longer expect assistance from the French
in their wars against the British.

To prepare the way for Bradstreet's arrival
Sir William Johnson had gone in advance to
Niagara, where he had called together ambassadors from all the tribes, not only from
those that had taken part in the war, but from
all within his jurisdiction. He had found
a vast concourse of Indians awaiting him.
The wigwams of over a thousand warriors
dotted the low-lying land at the mouth of the
river. In a few days the number had grown
to two thousand—representatives of nations
as far east as Nova Scotia, as far west as the

Mississippi, and as far north as Hudson Bay. Pontiac was absent, nor were there any Delaware, Shawnee, or Seneca ambassadors present. These were absent through dread ; but later the Senecas sent deputies to ratify the treaty made with Johnson in April. When Bradstreet and his troops arrived negotiations were in full swing. For nearly a month councils were held, and at length all the chiefs present had entered into an alliance with the British. This accomplished, Johnson, on August 6, left Niagara for his home, while Bradstreet continued his journey towards Detroit.

Bradstreet halted at Presqu'isle. Here he was visited by pretended deputies from the Shawnees and Delawares, who ostensibly sought peace. He made a conditional treaty with them and agreed to meet them twenty-five days later at Sandusky, where they were to bring their British prisoners. From Presqu'isle he wrote to Bouquet at Fort Pitt, saying that it would be unnecessary to advance into the Delaware country, as the Delawares were now at peace. He also reported his success, as he considered it, to Gage, but Gage was not impressed : he disavowed the treaty and instructed Bouquet to continue his pre-

parations. Continuing his journey, Bradstreet
rested at Sandusky, where more Delawares
waited on him and agreed to make peace. It
was at this juncture that he sent Captain
Thomas Morris on his ill-starred mission to
the tribes of the Mississippi.[1]

Bradstreet was at Detroit by August 26,
and at last the worn-out garrison of the fort
could rest after fifteen months of exacting
duties. Calling the Indians to a council, Bradstreet entered into treaties with a number of
chiefs, and pardoned several French settlers
who had taken an active part with the Indians
in the siege of Detroit. He then sent troops
to occupy Michilimackinac, Green Bay, and
Sault Ste Marie ; and sailed for Sandusky to
meet the Delawares and Shawnees, who had
promised to bring in their prisoners. But
none awaited him: the Indians had deliber-
ately deceived him and were playing for time

[1] Morris and his companions got no farther than the rapids
of the Maumee, where they were seized, stripped of clothing, and
threatened with death. Pontiac was now among the Miamis,
still striving to get together a following to continue the war.
The prisoners were taken to Pontiac's camp. But the Ottawa
chief did not deem it wise to murder a British officer on this
occasion, and Morris was released and forced to retrace his
steps. He arrived at Detroit after the middle of September,
only to find that Bradstreet had already departed. The story
will be found in more detail in Parkman's *Conspiracy of Pontiac*.

while they continued their attacks on the border settlers. Here he received a letter from Gage ordering him to disregard the treaty he had made with the Delawares and to join Bouquet at Fort Pitt, an order which Bradstreet did not obey, making the excuse that the low state of the water in the rivers made impossible an advance to Fort Pitt. On October 18 he left Sandusky for Niagara, having accomplished nothing except occupation of the forts. Having already blundered hopelessly in dealing with the Indians, he was to blunder still further. On his way down Lake Erie he encamped one night, when storm threatened, on an exposed shore, and a gale from the north-east broke upon his camp and destroyed half his boats. Two hundred and eighty of his soldiers had to march overland to Niagara. Many of them perished ; others, starved, exhausted, frost-bitten, came staggering in by twos and threes till near the end of December. The expedition was a fiasco. It blasted Bradstreet's reputation, and made the British name for a time contemptible among the Indians.

The other expedition from Fort Pitt has a different history. All through the summer Bouquet had been recruiting troops for the

invasion of the Delaware country. The soldiers were slow in arriving, and it was not
until the end of September that all was
ready. Early in October Bouquet marched
out of Fort Pitt with one thousand pro-
vincials and five hundred regulars. Crossing
the Alleghany, he made his way in a north-
westerly direction until Beaver Creek was
reached, and then turned westward into the
unbroken forest. The Indians of the Muskingum valley felt secure in their wilderness fast-
ness. No white soldiers had ever penetrated
to their country. To reach their villages
dense woods had to be penetrated, treacherous marshes crossed, and numerous streams
bridged or forded. But by the middle of
October Bouquet had led his army, without
the loss of a man, into the heart of the Muskingum valley, and pitched his camp near an
Indian village named Tuscarawa, from which
the inhabitants had fled at his approach.
The Delawares and Shawnees were terrified :
the victor of Edge Hill was among them with
an army strong enough to crush to atoms
any war-party they could muster. They sent
deputies to Bouquet. These at first assumed
a haughty mien ; but Bouquet sternly re-
buked them and ordered them to meet him

at the forks of the Muskingum, forty miles distant to the south-west, and to bring in all their prisoners. By the beginning of November the troops were at the appointed place, where they encamped. Bouquet then sent messengers to all the tribes telling them to bring thither all the captives without delay. Every white man, woman, and child in their hands, French or British, must be delivered up. After some hesitation the Indians made haste to obey. About two hundred captives were brought, and chiefs were left as hostages for the safe delivery of others still in the hands of distant tribes. So far Bouquet had been stern and unbending; he had reminded the Indians of their murder of settlers and of their black treachery regarding the garrisons, and hinted that except for the kindness of their British father they would be utterly destroyed. He now unbent and offered them a generous treaty, which was to be drawn up and arranged later by Sir William Johnson. Bouquet then retraced his steps to Fort Pitt, and arrived there on November 28 with his long train of released captives. He had won a victory over the Indians greater than his triumph at Edge Hill, and all the greater in that it was achieved without striking a blow.

There was still, however, important work to be done before any guarantee of permanent peace in the hinterland was possible. On the eastern bank of the Mississippi, within the country ceded to England by the Treaty of Paris, was an important settlement over which the French flag still flew, and to which no British troops or traders had penetrated. It was a hotbed of conspiracy. Even while Bouquet was making peace with the tribes between the Ohio and Lake Erie, Pontiac and his agents were trying to make trouble for the British among the Indians of the Mississippi.

French settlement on the Mississippi began at the village of Kaskaskia, eighty-four miles north of the mouth of the Ohio. Six miles still farther north was Fort Chartres, a strongly built stone fort capable of accommodating three hundred men. From here, at some distance from the river, ran a road to Cahokia, a village situated nearly opposite the site of the present city of St Louis. The intervening country was settled by prosperous traders and planters who, including their four hundred negro slaves, numbered not less than two thousand. But when it was learned that all the territory east of the great river had been

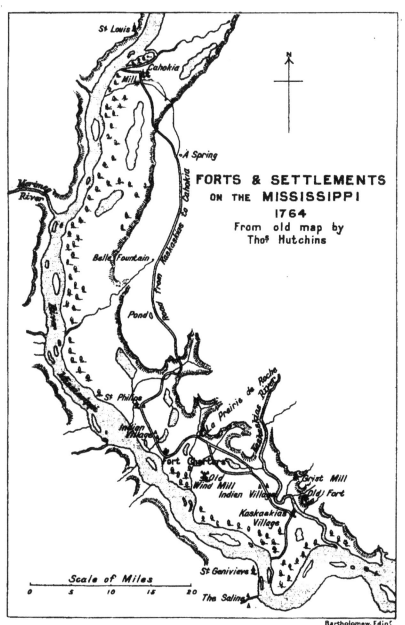

St. Louis

Cahokia

Mill

A Spring

FORTS & SETTLEMENTS
ON THE **MISSISSIPPI**
1764
From old map by
Thos Hutchins

Marine
River

Belle Fountain

Road from Kaskaskias to Cahokia

Pond

St Philips

Indian
Village

La Prairie de Roche

Kaskaskias River

Fort Chartres

Old
Wind Mill

Indian Village

Grist Mill

Old Fort

Kaskaskias
Village

St Genivieve

Scale of Miles

0   5   10   15   20

The Saline

Bartholomew, Edinr

ceded to Britain, the settlers began to migrate to the opposite bank. The French here were hostile to the incoming British, and feared lest they might now lose the profitable trade with New Orleans. It was this region that Gage was determined to occupy.

Already an effort had been made to reach Fort Chartres. In February 1764 Major Arthur Loftus had set out from New Orleans with four hundred men; but, when about two hundred and forty miles north of his starting-point, his two leading boats were fired upon by Indians. Six men were killed and four wounded. To advance would mean the destruction of his entire company. Loftus returned to New Orleans, blaming the French officials for not supporting his enterprise, and indeed hinting that they were responsible for the attack. Some weeks later Captain Philip Pittman arrived at New Orleans with the intention of ascending the river; but reports of the enmity of the Indians to the British made him abandon the undertaking. So at the beginning of 1765 the French flag still flew over Fort Chartres; and Saint-Ange, who had succeeded Neyon de Villiers as commandant of the fort, was praying that the British might soon arrive to relieve him from a position where he was being daily importuned by Pontiac or his emissaries for aid against what they called the common foe.

But, if the route to Fort Chartres by way of New Orleans was too dangerous, Bouquet had cleared the Ohio of enemies, and the country which Gage sought to occupy was now accessible by way of that river. As a preliminary step, George Croghan was sent in advance with presents for the Indians along the route. In May 1765 Croghan left Fort Pitt accompanied by a few soldiers and a number of friendly Shawnee and Delaware chiefs. Near the mouth of the Wabash a prowling band of Kickapoos attacked the party, killing several and making prisoners of the rest. Croghan and his fellow-prisoners were taken to the French traders at Vincennes, where they were liberated. They then went to Ouiatanon, where Croghan held a council, and induced many chiefs to swear fealty to the British. After leaving Ouiatanon, Croghan had proceeded westward but a little way when he was met by Pontiac with a number of chiefs and warriors. At last the arch-conspirator was ready to come to terms. The French on the Mississippi would give him no assistance. He realized now that his people were conquered,

and before it was too late he must make peace
with his conquerors. Croghan had no further
reason to continue his journey; so, accompanied by Pontiac, he went to Detroit. Arriving there on August 17, he at once called a
council of the tribes in the neighbourhood.
At this council sat Pontiac, among chiefs
whom he had led during the months of the
siege of Detroit. But it was no longer the
same Pontiac : his haughty, domineering spirit
was broken; his hopes of an Indian empire
were at an end. ' Father,' he said at this
council, ' I declare to all nations that I had
made my peace with you before I came
here ; and I now deliver my pipe to Sir
William Johnson, that he may know that I
have made peace, and taken the king of
England to be my father in the presence of
all the nations now assembled.' He further
agreed to visit Oswego in the spring to con-
clude a treaty with Sir William Johnson himself. The path was now clear for the advance
of the troops to Fort Chartres. As soon as
news of Croghan's success reached Fort Pitt,
Captain Thomas Sterling, with one hundred
and twenty men of the Black Watch, set out
in boats for the Mississippi, arriving on
October 9 at Fort Chartres, the first British

troops to set foot in that country. Next day
Saint-Ange handed the keys of the fort to
Sterling, and the Union Jack was flung aloft.
Thus, nearly three years after the signing
of the Treaty of Paris, the fleurs-de-lis dis-
appeared from the territory then known as
Canada.

There is still to record the closing act in
the public career of Pontiac. Sir William
Johnson, fearing that the Ottawa chief might
fail to keep his promise of visiting Oswego
to ratify the treaty made with Croghan at
Detroit, sent Hugh Crawford, in March 1766,
with belts and messages to the chiefs of
the Ottawa Confederacy. But Pontiac was
already preparing for his journey eastward.
Nothing in his life was more creditable than
his bold determination to attend a council far
from his hunting-ground, at which he would
be surrounded by soldiers who had suffered
treachery and cruelty at his hands—whose
comrades he had tortured and murdered.

On July 23 there began at Oswego the grand
council at which Sir William Johnson and
Pontiac were the most conspicuous figures.
For three days the ceremonies and speeches
continued ; and on the third day Pontiac rose
in the assembly and made a promise that he

was faithfully to keep: ' I take the Great Spirit to witness,' he said, ' that what I am going to say I am determined steadfastly to perform. . . . While I had the French king by the hand, I kept a fast hold of it ; and now having you, father, by the hand, I shall do the same in conjunction with all the western nations in my district.'

Before the council ended Johnson presented to each of the chiefs a silver medal engraved with the words: ' A pledge of peace and friendship with Great Britain, confirmed in 1766.' He also loaded Pontiac and his brother chiefs with presents ; then, on the last day of July, the Indians scattered to their homes.

For three years Pontiac, like a restless spirit, moved from camp to camp and from hunting-ground to hunting-ground. There were outbreaks of hostilities in the Indian country, but in none of these did he take part. His name never appears in the records of those three years. His days of conspiracy were at an end. By many of the French and Indians he was distrusted as a pensioner of the British, and by the British traders and settlers he was hated for his past deeds. In 1769 he visited the Mississippi, and while at Cahokia he attended a drunken frolic held by some Indians. When he left the feast, stupid from the effects of rum, he was followed into the forest by a Kaskaskia Indian, probably bribed by a British trader. And as Pontiac lurched among the black shadows of the trees, his pursuer crept up behind him, and with a swift stroke of the tomahawk cleft his skull. Thus by a treacherous blow ended the career of a warrior whose chief weapon had been treachery.

For twelve years England, by means of military officers, ruled the great hinterland east of the Mississippi—a region vast and rich, which now teems with a population immensely greater than that of the whole broad Dominion of Canada—a region which is to-day dotted with such magnificent cities as Chicago, Detroit, and Indianapolis. Unhappily, England made no effort to colonize this wilderness empire. Indeed, as Edmund Burke has said, she made ' an attempt to keep as a lair of wild beasts that earth which God, by an express charter, had given to the children of men.' She forbade settlement in the hinterland. She did this ostensibly for the Indians, but in reality for the merchants in the mother country. In a report of the

Lords Commissioners for Trade and Plantations in 1772 are words which show that it was the intention of the government to confine ' the western extent of settlements to such a distance from the seaboard as that those settlements should lie within easy reach of the trade and commerce of this kingdom, . . . and also of the exercise of that authority and jurisdiction . . . necessary for the preservation of the colonies in a due subordination to, and dependence upon, the mother country. . . . It does appear to us that the extension of the fur trade depends entirely upon the Indians being undisturbed in the possession of their hunting-grounds. . . . Let the savages enjoy their deserts in quiet. Were they driven from their forests the peltry trade would decrease, and it is not impossible that worse savages would take refuge in them.'

Much has been written about the stamp tax and the tea tax as causes of the American revolution, but this determination to confine the colonies to the Atlantic seaboard ' rendered the revolution inevitable.' [1] In 1778, three years after the sword was drawn, when an American force under George Rogers Clark invaded the Indian country, England's weakly

[1] Roosevelt's *The Winning of the West*, part i, p. 57.

garrisoned posts, then by the Quebec Act under the government of Canada, were easily captured ; and, when accounts came to be settled after the war, the entire hinterland south of the Great Lakes, from the Alleghanies to the Mississippi, passed to the United States.

BIBLIOGRAPHICAL NOTE

THE main source of information regarding the siege of Detroit is the 'Pontiac Manuscript.' This work has been translated several times, the best and most recent translation being that by R. Clyde Ford for the *Journal of Pontiac's Conspiracy, 1763*, edited by C. M. Burton. Unfortunately, the manuscript abruptly ends in the middle of the description of the fight at Bloody Run.

The following works will be found of great assistance to the student: Rogers's *Journals*; Cass's *Discourse before the Michigan Historical Society*; Henry's *Travels and Adventures in Canada and the Indian Territories*; Parkman's *Conspiracy of Pontiac* (the fullest and best treatment of the subject); Ellis's *Life of Pontiac, the Conspirator* (a digest of Parkman's work); *Historical Account of the Expedition against the Ohio Indians, 1764* (authorship doubtful, but probably written by Dr William Smith of Philadelphia); Stone's *The Life and Times of Sir William Johnson*; Drake's *Indians of North America*; *Handbook of American Indians North of Mexico* and *Handbook of Indians of Canada*; Ogg's *The Opening of the Mississippi*; Roosevelt's *The Winning of the West*; Carter's *The Illinois Country*; Beer's *British Colonial Policy, 1754-1765*;

Adair's *The History of the American Indians*; the *Annual Register* for the years 1763, 1764, and 1774; Harper's *Encyclopedia of United States History*; Pownall's *The Administration of the Colonies*; Bancroft's *History of the United States*; Kingsford's *History of Canada*; Winsor's *Narrative and Critical History of America* and his *Mississippi Basin*; Gordon's *History of Pennsylvania*; Lucas's *A History of Canada, 1763-1812*; Gayarré's *History of Louisiana*; and M'Master's *History of the People of the United States*.

In 1766 there was published in London a somewhat remarkable drama entitled *Ponteach : or the Savages of America*. A part of this will be found in the appendices to Parkman's *Conspiracy of Pontiac*. Parkman suggests that Robert Rogers may have had a hand in the composition of this drama.

INDEX

Amherst, Sir Jeffery, in command of the British forces in America, 7, 18, 24, 25, 28, 121; his opinion and tactless treatment of the Indians, 7-8, 30-1, 32; at last aroused, 62, 94-5, 106, 115.

Bâby, Jacques, provisions Fort Detroit, 51-2, 56, 64.
Beaver War, the, 16. See Pontiac War.
Belêtre, Sieur de, hands over Fort Detroit to Rogers, 21-3 and note.
Black Watch (42nd Highlanders), the, 95, 99, 100-1, 103-5; at Fort Chartres, 133.
Blane, Lieut. Archibald, his defence of Fort Ligonier, 97, 122.
Bloody Run, battle of, 63-7.
Bocquet, Father, at Fort Detroit, 40.
Bouquet, Colonel Henry, his opinion of the Indians, 7-8, 30; his relief expedition to Fort Pitt, 88, 94, 95, 96-9, 105-6, 125, 127; his victories at Bushy Run and Edge Hill, 99-105; his bloodless victory over the Delawares and Shawnees, 127-9; a great soldier, 95, 101-2, 106, 122.
Braddock, General, his dis-

aster at Duquesne, 94, 98, 102, 106.
Bradstreet, Colonel John, his disastrous expedition, 123-7.
Brant, Joseph, the Mohawk chief, 123.
British in America, their sad plight, 87. See Great Britain and Thirteen Colonies.
Burke, Edmund, his criticism of Britain's colonial policy, 136.
Bushy Run, battle of, 98-100.

Campau, Louis, French settler at Detroit, 59, 60.
Campbell, Captain Donald, at Fort Detroit, 22, 23, 46; reveals an Indian plot, 24; kept prisoner by Pontiac, 49-50, 53; murdered, 61, 70.
Canada, after the Conquest, 6-7, 18-19.
Chapoton, Jean Baptiste, his mission to Pontiac, 48-9.
Chevalier, Louis, his valuable services at Fort St Joseph, 72.
Chesne, Miny, assists Indians at Fort Miami, 74.
Chesne, Pierre. See La Butte.
Chippewas, the, 12, 13, 34, 39, 42, 46, 47, 61, 67, 77-9, 80-1, 82, 114.
Christie, Ensign John, his sur-

141

Printed by T. and A. Constable, Printers to His Majesty
at the Edinburgh University Press

Printed in the USA
CPSIA information can be obtained
at www.ICGtesting.com
CBHW080119010224
3926CB00005B/198

9 781020 627330